CONTRITION

Clear Waters For Troubled Souls

OMAR ZAID, MD

Contrition: Clear Waters For Troubled Souls

Copyright © 2025 by Omar Zaid, MD

aka: *Leonard Joseph Owsiany Jr*
ISBN- 979-8-9925010-0-1 eBook
ISBN- 979-8-9925010-1-8 Print
All rights reserved.

No part of this book may be reproduced in any form or by any electronic or mechanical means, including information storage and retrieval systems, without written permission from the author, except for the use of brief quotations in a book review or academic reference.

Cover Design by Dr Omar & Amina Qun Gu,
using elements from Salvador Dali's LAST SUPPER

https://alginkgo.com/
info@algikgo.com

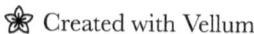 Created with Vellum

*For Sojourners
Who Know Their Worth*

🔑 *I shall never rest until I have undone the harm I did to so many well-meaning, innocent Negroes who, through my own evangelistic zeal, now believe in him even more fanatically and more blindly than I did.*

Malcolm-X

THE CENSOR

intro by dr zaid

I knew Malcolm was murdered for disclosing artifice at NOI's helm, but until undertaking this research I did not understand 'why' his life was forfeit under heaven's eye, especially before his renaissance took root. The answer helped me to comprehend why bad things happen to good people. To clarify this and other points of spiritual law, I share what has since been brought to my attention; especially for anyone with more intimate knowledge of events that precipitated this account. Indeed, among them are souls who can personally have a hand in attending to the unfinished business of Malcolm's reform.

Writing this was an instructive grapple with the American psyche that nearly buried my novel and marriage for nine months. It compelled me until its waters broke in mid Dec of 2024, which is when I learned of the new lawsuit. A convenient coincidence? An omen? — Indeed, the NOI experience proves a useful tool that helps us clarify why chastity and contrition assist our conscious reunification with divine will as garments of G-d consciousness

(Q.21.80). My struggle's brief has become a cautionary moral lesson for all, but most especially for those who defend premises that constitute institutional integrity (Q.4.17-18). Thank you for taking the time.

In sum, I believe infidelity's betrayal of trust was at the core of why the right honorable Malcom-X was murdered. The apocalypse that preceded his demise showed that *Fard & Poole Ltd.* were but a cog in the fraternal wheels of pied-piping conmen who've been piping globally for quite some time. You know the type; they marshal walking dead-folks into noisome parades for profit. Taken together they comprise *The Man Of Sin* or *Mystery of Iniquity* spoken of in scripture (2.Thess.1-7). Brother Malcolm faithfully, effectively, fearlessly, and serially indicted them all. This is why he was killed. NOI may have driven that bus but they didn't own it.

This book describes the fruits of fidelity versus infidelity. The former owns chaste initiates who phase-transition in lock step with evolution. They are transfigured by conscious ascendance to divine will, and well know that adultery is far more than a mere retreat from faithful well dipping. History proves it, and when properly read, scripture teaches that infidelity initiates a default death-processing algorithm that morbidly and autonomously causes the dissolution of human purpose. This specifically occurs when we unilaterally divorce our will from moral turpitude.

I write with foreboding because men prefer tectonic myths to the blood, sweat, and tears of authentic history. My study of our ancient school of dissimulation began in the cradle. For much of 2023 and into early 2024, it involved regular online discussions with several folks, some of whom failed to disclose devotions to preposterous cosmological, theological, eschatological, and archeological doctrines; including flat-earth mania, alien-friendly global mudslides, and a profane book of hagiography that would make St Peter cringe. While professing Islam, they cautiously kept concealed designs and affiliations with *The Nation of Islam* in the caboose.

The curtain was fortuitously removed in February of 2024. Chagrined but intensely curious, I ended our palavers and re-read NOI history, only to confirm suspicions I held twenty-five years previously. Chief among these was that the right honorable Malcolm-X's life was cut short by a gang of poseurs. But I discovered far more.

After accepting the commission of nemesis, I learned that NOI's trans-evaluation of the American Negro was no mere episode or commercial break, but rather a re-branding effort made by sponsors of a hoary mythology that subverts authentic cultural mores. Its hue and cry is no call to "*Strength & Honor*" but rather that of the organized barbarity that has so far attended sixty-odd centuries of highborn rapine; the very same that recently rebranded America's Great Turtle. The conspiracy is that old.

What remains after deep cultural subversion is a dispirited carcass of vehemently expansive gloom whose phantoms attend to fate but not destiny. A goodly portion of this is achieved by the insidious thirst for fame and booty that Schiller attributed to '*bread-fed scholars who cut asunder an organic whole till it lay in tatters.*' Substitute *You-tube* for *bread* and you get the picture.

Fard & Poole Ltd's *tour de force* was thus a chutzpa extravaganza of colossal arrogance noised abroad by bread-fed barkers. It still and confidently buoys the illusion of self-determination by raising a chauvinist obelisk with practiced guile. Disciples swallow its swill and swillers with patient anticipationa only to resurrect pious savagery when the pot of lies is threatened.

Sadly, brother Malcolm's demise proved an unhappy birthright; one that confirms scripture and several cited arguments below. His death rings a moment of silence that proves the law of regression, which, like the prophetic slap described by Robert Graves in *King Jesus*, ever lays in wait for its punishing moment. In this new light we see Malcolm indelibly cuffed to cruel brutes under the weight of corrupt oaths. With G-d's help, I explain why such gangs haplessly and publicly founder in the absence of contrition.

My arguments draw on eschatological absolutes supported by sciences that yield a more sober theology. I approach a unified field of synthesis by employing mimesis with singular scriptural insights that remove what would otherwise remain a veiled history joined to errant exegesis on both sides of the Nile. Using testimonies from participants and sober sleuths, my cautionary essays criticize mountebanks who live to misguide anyone who prefers rose colored myths.

Fundamental matters concern the sweeping sociopolitical and spiritual implications of infidelity, especially on social constructs that fashion ideas that are used to construct the metabolic mesenchyme and grist of communities that enable criminals to rule. Hence, this is an exercise in what Dr A Łobaczewski called *Ponerology*, and what Professor William Connolly described as neuro-politics. [1]

I have learned that infidelity at the helm of social institutions is no light matter because chaste conjugal unions

---

1. https://forum.alginkgo.com/go/Yvucrzl9fJ

obtain the supernal guidance and protection that Muslims call, *rahim grace*. The New Testament calls it *life more abundantly* (John.10.10). Because these essays attempt to show how it is accomplished, with divine help I hope to leave no doubt as to the furtive genesis or roguish goals of NOI founders. Like Pharisees, they prevent the incarnation of the Kingdom's dominion. My disclosures are, therefore, a kind of forensic investigation that takes Malcolm's indictments a step further by making it exceptionally clear that *Fard & Poole Ltd.* did not and could not possibly have obtained celestial imprimatur.

I am the censor who reveals an unsuspected path; one that is that is commonly trod by magical thinkers, especially since Alexander taught Caesar to adopt and adapt its delusional ring of power for neuro-political purposes. More stoic disciplines that forbid such vulgar sensationalism, on the other hand, represent what gospels call 'good-fruit'. NOI has certainly showed potential as a disciplined lot of hardy souls. Even so, I suggest their saplings cannot yet be set in the enriched soil that marks high cultural maturity. I say this because healthy growth requires resilient components designed for systemic applications that inhabit and support reiterative patterns of healthy development. As the reader will learn, such resilience affords virile foundations and cornerstones that radiate virtue at existential quantum levels.

INTRO BY DR ZAID

🗝 *Dictum*: Untainted fractals exude the applied wisdom that follows all clear water baptisms. Thus, an ongoing stream is required to actively command a sojourner's faithful navigation. Otherwise slavery ensues.

Therefore: When lost, CONTRITION precedes all claims to the sagacity required to reset mankind's errant compass?

It is clear that Brother Malcolm-X was throughly shriven and then given the mace of moral authority. Designated survivors and NOI-friendly collectives are herein urged to experience the winnowing grace of his prodigal reconciliation because it is the only processing that accesses unpolluted trans-dimensional conduits of supernal grace. I cannot state this spiritual law any clearer than that. But I will attempt to share its scientifically proven flux as a dynamic process of etheric waters that proceed from unseen realms, much like opening drapes and windows to allow more light and fresh air into the soul's closed room.² Seen or unseen, public or private, individual or corporate, I will show how fidelity ushers the immaculate radiance that cleanses and restores worn and weary temples, and naturally maintains a posture of worshipful obedience for all who acknowledge divine order.

Steadfast devotion (fidelity) teaches us how to sift, sort, process, eat, save, protect, and plant good seed in chaste soil. It is how the earth winnows its inmates. Truth liberates by allowing unadulterated life-giving waters to flow through unseen, inter-dimensional channels. This circulation of immaculate *plasma* purchases the gnostic alchemy that transforms us into *"little gods"* who correctly discern right from wrong. Thus, sagacious percipience marks all prophets and their disciples as intimate companions of *The Great Mystery*. Anything else is the rhetorical nonsense that keeps magical thinkers bound to gilded podiums, blood sacrifice, and filthy lucre, all of which took Malcolm from us. You should be hearing this from him.

This book magnifies this good man's memory by explaining why marital fidelity is the cure. The reader will learn that unseen hands set Elijah Poole's cornerstone of infidelity on massive blocks of accretion filled with vain premises. Any structured denial of his moral failings and bungled erudition forensically describes those who commonly reject truth in deference to spell-binding neologisms and hagiographies that shroud many a fouled temple and mausoleum.

So let the apocalypse begin and the nation return. And,

---

2. See ***Sexology For The Wise***: Noetic Science, Intro To The New Physics https://forum.alginkgo.com/go/WT65DjLFk5

INTRO BY DR ZAID

G-d willing, let the name of Malcolm-X be honorably remembered.

THE PRINCE HALL PLOT

by Sister Klara,
a worthy Indonesian sister

This is based on testimony given by Sheikh Imran Nazar Hosein, who personally knew Betty Shabazz, Malcolm's wife, and his daughter, Qubilah. Before relating the plot orchestrated by COINTELPRO agents and NOI thugs, it is important to note that Louis Farrakhan was a 32nd degree Prince Hall Freemason. Stalwarts such as Professor John Robison; British historian, Nesta Webster; Captain William Guy Carr of the Royal Canadian Navy; Lady Edith Starr Miller of Queenborough; and our respected teachers, Dr Omar Zaid, and the intrepid JT Bard, along with numerous others, have recorded the history of this subversion which precedes even that of the Babylonian Talmud that governs all such lodges.

Malcolm-X's free-spirit could not betray his inborn nature, so it wasn't long before he realized that NOI's racist cult gave Black Americans a mere promise of Islam by

THE PRINCE HALL PLOT

saying it was a religion 'for black people only'. Knowingly misguiding their followers as did the Qarmathian Al Hajjaj Al Tsaqafi during the time of Abdallah ibn Zubayr, NOI leaders presented inner-city negroes with volumes of outrageous nonsense, claiming all was verified truth. They even claimed Mohammad Ali spoke to G-d on the phone daily to confirm their authority.

After visiting Mecca, Malcolm realized the scam. He then raised a challenge that we in Indonesia call '*kalimatu adl indha sultani jair*', or *words of justice thrown at a tyrant*. Because he exposed the organized corruption of this "*gang*", Malcolm was murdered. They even made sure he was buried far from his beloved Harlem. Sheikh Imran Hosein said they did this to erase both his memory and work of reform. But Malcolm's wife, Betty Shabazz, kept his legacy alive. She even unabashedly corrected Sheikh Imran who once criticized Malcolm for not understanding the evils of usury; proudly proclaiming, "*My husband didn't die on riba!*"

Betty Shabazz and Malcolm's children saw him assassinated. Without exception, they all claimed Louis Farrakhan was the mastermind. Malcolm's daughter, Qubilah, had studied at the Sorbonne and had an Algerian lover with whom she had a son. The affair ended and she returned to the States. Soon afterwards she was honey-trapped by an FBI informant named Michael Fitzpatrick, whom she told of her plan to assassinate Mr. Farrakhan. This confession was then used to blackmail her and her mother in NOI's favor. Betty Shabazz did everything possible to free her daughter from their grip, otherwise Ms Q could have been jailed for decades.

Sheikh Imran lamented the backdoor deal, especially after Ms Shabazz and Mr Farrakhan made a show of reconciliation to end the schism. Many suspect it was to avoid further exposure of NOI corruption and its incriminating ties to persons known and unknown.

At the time, Malcolm Shabazz, a troubled child and son of Ms Q, was ten years old and in the care of Ms. Shabazz, his grandmother. For reasons unknown, he set her apartment on fire, severely injuring her. Ms Shabazz died. He pled guilty and was detained in a juvenile correctional facility. Sheikh Imran regretted never visiting him as a father figure. Years later, at the age of 28, Malcolm Shabazz died during a bar fight in Mexico City.

Dr Zaid says outcomes like these are inevitably caused by infidelities that cause hell to fall on those who misplace their trust. His exceptionally lucid analysis takes up the cause of Malcolm-X by explaining why contrition is necessary (Q.24.10).

(Indonesia, 2024)

~ The Honorable Baba Shuaib ~
ALLAH'S CORRECTIONS OFFICIER

Malcolm X was an influential figure in Black American history, known for his powerful voice advocating for civil rights and social justice. He became a prominent leader of the *Nation of Islam* from his troubled youth, and later became a global human rights activist who reflected the complexities of race relations in the United States. He challenged the status quo and urged African Americans to take pride in their heritage and fight against oppression. He also urged them to become true Muslims and have respect for all races. This book highlights his enduring legacy and emphasizes the importance of standing up for justice and equality in our own times.

1

THE OYSTER'S PEARL
INDICTMENTS

you are what you eat

🔍 After Malcolm's "divorce" from the Nation of Islam, a new picture of Elijah Muhammad begins to emerge. Malcolm's disillusionment was partially due to Muhammad's unfaithfulness to his own moral codes. It becomes increasingly clear that Elijah Muhammad is nothing more than a self-serving hypocrite, feeding off the false hopes of his followers ... The final impression of Elijah Muhammad is of a cunning old man who will stop at nothing, including the murder of his most faithful and trusted lieutenant.

Shepard, Ray. CliffsNotes on The Autobiography of Malcom X.

THE CONSCIOUS CONSTRUCTION of the human persona and its cooperatives occurs in developmental stages, as do the designs of Operative Freemasonry. Both stand at the Adamic core of things scriptural. The individual and social engineering espoused as sacred is based on disciplines that enable our best understanding and use of science and language. It is the stone upon which Moses and Joshua found Al' Khidr sitting. The same initiation found Abraham's Melchizedek, as well as Moses, Mohammad, Halaj, and The Son of Miriam (Rumi: *Mathnawi #290*).*

Those who die to self resurrect in the house of G-d; *in-the-world* but *not-of-it,* and seek alliance with morally upright folks everywhere. Knowing them by their fruit embodies crafts and skills mastered by our best architects, mathematicians, philosophers, scientists, musicians, artisans and engineers. Ideally, they are properly informed colleges of people who know how best to obtain and maintain morally operative order for the benefit of all and to the exclusion of evil.[1] This last condition specifically excludes charismatic liars who cheat on their wives. Rumi describes them as insolent scoundrels living in borrowed robes (*Mathnawi* #670).

In sum, this brief proposes the following:

1. That NOI leaders remain in collusion with Deep State redactors; noting that FBI, sundry secret services, police, and immigration agencies, still refuse to cooperate fully with historians and other researchers regarding NOI records.
2. In addition to surviving an extremely suspect genesis, NOI leaders bequeathed a syncretic mass of befuddling cosmology and theology mired in capital crimes.
3. NOI founders were Dark Personalities whose wolfish sadomasochism consumed the substance

---

1. * See "Until The Eschaton Is Spent" Sep 2024 https://forum.alginkgo.com/go/V4-LbsAqlE

and lives of unprotected sheep. (Chap 3-8; Appendices: *Psychopath Profile Notes*)

Transsexuals confirm this last indictment by example because it typifies a character trait of predators who disassociate from truth and proceed to destroy those of their genus who expose their lies. They openly express psychopathology by placing trust in a delusion, and do so at any and all costs to others. This coherent description also fits confirmed hypocrisy and describes designated survivors stamped '*good fruit mixed with bad*', the tree of which Adam was commanded not to eat. Before ruffling your feathers consider that eating forbidden fruit, when it's the only food available, becomes tradition, which in no way improves seed quality. Nature is then obliged to wall it off or expel it.

Brother Malcom exclusively ate NOI rations until he noticed grave contradistinctions learned by experience. This is but one of several reasons Warith Mohammad heroically whitewashed his father's legacy of lies with universal principles. Sadly, in the eternal scheme of things that matter, white-washing a cornerstone full of lies merely makes the dead bones of duplicity within it acceptable. Once entrenched, contrition is never again considered by permanently biased inspectors and duped pawns caught in the downspout of its dark gyrus.

🗝 Such a lapse in erudite scrutiny prevents the correction of errors that must be acknowledged before grace is restored and troops are moved to the front. Nonetheless, in G-d's infinite wisdom it can also become the oyster's pearl when you call it what it is because it enslaves you until you own it.

mysteries & forests

Like the mysteries of Orpheus, NOI's foundational worldview planks were cut from *Nisari-Ismaili* forests where Mani and Nimrud once hunted the souls of men. This doesn't mean much to our majority, but not a few initiatory protocols were adapted for game-play on Speculative Freemasonry's board and should never be attributed to Operative Freemasons. This depreciation of the ideal mostly occurred under Adam Weishaupt, a Jesuit master-infiltrator who borrowed these algorithms from Ibn Maymun; the Yazidi magus of Jewish extraction out of Kurdistan who fathered the notorious Fatimid cult.

In sum, the Left-Hand Path of Persian Mysteries (think *Three Wise Men*)—derives from pre-Judaic Kabbalists married to debased Medes and Zoroastrians who studied *Harut* & *Marut*'s graduate program for politically correct *Gog* & *Magog* management systems. All hail from Babylon's child sacrificing basin in unclean Promised Lands. Which, by the way, includes much of modern Syria, especially the Golan, and extends far north.[2]

Popular cults have regally dressed Right-Hand Path managerial boards of organized religion in the semiotics that inform much of this pedantic misguidance. On this magog side of the divide, they perennially re-organize doctrinal positions pinned to numerous corrupt translations of scripture, along with misinterpretations and base inter-

---

[2.] See: ***Cain's Creed*** https://forum.alginkgo.com/go/rS-iVukcgS

*** SF Dunlap, (1894) ***Ghebers of Hebron***, 1894 https://forum.alginkgo.com/go/dNsbYDs9yp

J E Katz (2001). History of the Kurds (impossible to find now), if anyone does, please let me know.

that favor Zionism, the Internationale's codeword for Organized Elitist Plunder.

Modern bloodlines claiming to be Lilly of the Valley legatees use the Jesuit *fleur-de-lis* as an identifier (Appendices: *Annunaki*). Over time, this massive but more palatable bowl of word salad was moored to syncretic Rome and even Mecca (Appendices: *Subversion of Islam*). With great skill they re-introduced pagan mythology and reiteratively use it to prompt exceptional minions into killing and/or enslaving 'others' over the useless nonsense of noble lies.

With heaven's help I have plotted a course to the promised land of reason; hopefully, with repentant survivors in tow.

⚷ * JESUS AND JAMES were master architects according to Roman soldiers who left an oral tradition backed by documents that theologians commonly ignore. Mr. JT Bard, an oral historian with roots dating to Macedonia and beyond, assures me this tradition was bequeathed to *Operative Freemasons*.

⚷ THE LAMB OF G-D: The first mention of lambs being offered as substitute sacrifices for human babies is from Sumer, 3-4th BCE. See W Durant. *Our Oriental Heritage*

2

NOETIC CONTRITION
A SINGULAR EXEGESIS

genesis

IN KEEPING WITH NATIVE AMERICAN LORE, biblical writers figuratively and variously refer to redeemed humans as metonymic 'relatives' of *The Great Mystery* who return to their ancestors. In biblical terms, we are *"gathered to our fathers and mothers"* who have commonly been called, children of G-d.

> 🗝 Genesis 15:15 As for you [Abraham], you shall **go to your fathers** in peace; you will be buried at a good old age.
>
> Genesis 25:8 Abraham breathed his last and died in a ripe old age, an old man and satisfied with life; and he was **gathered to his people**.
>
> Genesis 35:29 Isaac breathed his last and died and was **gathered to his people**, an old man of ripe age; and his sons Esau and Jacob buried him.
>
> Genesis 49:29 I [Jacob] am about to be **gathered to my people**; bury me with my fathers in the cave that is in the field of Ephron the Hittite.
>
> Numbers 20:24 Aaron will be **gathered to his people**; for he shall not enter

the land which I have given to the sons of Israel, because you rebelled against My command at the waters of Meribah.

Judges 2:10 All that generation [Joshua's] also were **gathered to their fathers**; and there arose another generation after them who did not know the Lord, nor yet the work which He had done for Israel.

> Examples include
> bride or body -*of Christ* ... and
> son or daughter -*of G-d* or -*of Man*.
> 🔑 **Q.21.26-27** says they are *honored servants*

Everyone is somehow joined or married to a polity somewhere else called a son or daughter -*of god* or *of-man*. And those not considered G-d's kin are called *children of the devil*. Divine kin appear to have heaven's seal of approval with G-d either as *originator, father,* or *father-in-law*. All such clans are advised to turn in contrition for guidance, restoration, and protection every time they slip off the straight and narrow. These kinship references esoterically indicate the status of our transcendent soul: first as individuals and secondly as collectives (clannish or national zeitgeist). Nowhere is kinship status given to non-believers, especially in *Al'Qur'an*, which distinctly practices apartheid when it comes to the dispersion of rahim grace.

Gideon's praetorian guard and the People of Abraham are treated separately from Israel, which is called *Jacob's body* just as Christians are called the *body* of Christ. On it goes, and much to the chagrin of contemporary evangelicals. It seems OT prophets were called *sons-of*-G-d who judged their people much like a Cher'a'mon or Gypsy King (Appendices: *G-d's Relatives*). Simply put, metonymic relatives of G-d in Judeo-Christian traditions have a defined purpose and spiritual kinship with our Source Creator.

Expansive exegetic expositions are permitted and even encouraged; first because '*life is in the blood*', and secondly because G-d *Almighty* is the *Tree of Life* found in *Eden*—all of which terms have esoteric meanings. However, and I beg you to pause, these terms were never ever intended to be taken literally. Hence, post-modern evangelical carping to the contrary proves the tom-foolery of Lucifer's Right-Hand-Path under discussion.

For these and other well-substantiated reasons, I treat Elijah Poole as criminal in light of exegetic eschatology. Here the matter of *adultery* versus *fidelity* must be clearly understood in terms of gold-like purity, especially for those who take up the call of divine messaging. As the reader will learn, assigned scriptural attributions described as "clear waters" are indeed scientifically literal as well as metaphysically resonant. Such matters are explored below in terms of human access to supernal grace.

premises

> ___ 🗝 Monogamous fidelity is a kind of lightening rod that attracts and obtains the highest degree of trustworthy guidance.

> ___ 🗝 Monogamous fidelity exemplifies our singular relationship with G-d Almighty as agents, in unity, of divine authority.

> ___ 🗝 If true, then some humans metaphorically qualify as G-d's in-laws;

> ___ ▶ Adam being the first Son-of-God, ___ ▶ and Iesa (Jesus) being a son-of-G-d and son-of-man or Adam, i.e. the alpha and omega prophet for Jews, whose line was cut off due to gross idolatry, sexual perversion, and human sacrifice, especially in the Golan. ___ ▶ thus, when taken together, prophets and their people become divine consorts (a Caliphate, replete with shura and ummah).

Voltaire warned us that charismatic frauds cause many to believe in absurdities and commit atrocities. This describes Elijah Poole. His mentor, the enigmatic Master Fard, is on the Detroit police blotter admitting that he gamed Detroit ghetto dwellers who misplaced their trust in him. The magistrate accepted his confession and then *"exiled"* him and a few others for causing a riot involving more than 10,000 people. In addition to gaming, ritual murder and sacrifices made *"for the sake of the hereafter"* were popular voodoo themes during the gumshoe, hot-summer days that plagued NOI's back alleys during those years.[1]

In another essay collection, I show how and why conjugal morals are inextricably woven into human life so that marriage has everything to do with the evolution of trust and/or its misplacement.[2] Connubial obligations and etiquette, conscious and not, help us define the limits and duties of all trusts held with mutual benefits in view.

---

1. SEE: Beynon, E. D. (1938). The Voodoo Cult Among Negro Migrants in Detroit. American Journal of Sociology, 43(6), 894–907. http://www.jstor.org/stable/2768686
2. SEE: *TRUST*: Ontogeny Misplacement https://forum.alginkgo.com/go/8WkEa0Cp8Y
   Anita Teresa: Remedies for Narcissism, Sadism & Masochism https://forum.alginkgo.com/go/ncDYhBjAJc

Everyone knows that chaste monogamy stands sentinel over this cradle of civilization because any lesser degree of 'being' cannot attain divine *in-law* trust status. For this reason, chauvinist scribes tend to adjust their cant in favor of either polyamory or vain abstinence as superior paths for exceptional heroes of choice.

In addition to spiritual conundrums, at the time of Malcolm's epiphany, NOI opportunists struggled with sociological changes common to all institutions:

> 🔍 As an MO [movement organization] attains an economic and social base in society, as the original charismatic leadership is replaced, a bureaucratic structure emerges and a general accommodation to society occurs. Participants have a stake in preserving the organization, regardless of its ability to attain goals.
>
> 🔍 Analytically there are three types of changes involved in this process; empirically they are often fused: goal transformation; a shift to organizational maintenance; and oligarchization.

It seems NOI founders duplicitously corralled and misspent the hopes and resources of their disciples. Good faith trustworthiness is divinely intended to inhabit the clay of our being. Conmen know this and work hard to marshal its fervor in their favor. But even cons are dupes played by smarter fools. Which brings us to the pyramid's group pathology; that of neruo-politics:

🔍 Three changes began to appear the early 1960s:

> First: NOI's ideal and transcendental goals were transformed from the militant and revolutionary towards conservatism and material interests.
>
> Second: after attaining organizational and economic institutionalization, NOI tended to modify its beliefs and policies in close alignment with dominant societal norms.
>
> Third: NOI formed a centralized official hierarchy consisting of Elijah Poole's family and close relatives.

NOI's devolution involved community centers called *Temples,* whose administrators deferred to 'trust circles' approved by NOI's chief racketeers.[3] Islam's caliphs similarly practiced nepotism. It is a fatal flaw.

transcendent symmetry

We find slippery slopes on NOI's mystical facade in every direction. Any exceptional group's utopian venture has little operative value when reasonable contemplations penetrate horizons beyond their borders. The wisdom of not taking what belongs to others requires lying persuasiveness. It is a hard won prize. In NOI's case, profoundly ignorant souls were fleeced while myopically entertaining carpet rides through vast empty spaces of speculative cosmology.

To the contrary, Operative Freemasons are nobles who know they dwell in the sight of G-d and so honor all existential foci and refractions. No head-rocking, fez-topped

---

3. ibid, pp. 327-8; also see M. Parenti, Black Muslims: From Revolution to Institution, Social Research 31 (1964), 175-94. https://www.jstor.org/stable/40969726

* See: Trust, op.cit. https://forum.alginkgo.com/go/8WkEa0Cp8Y

bearded bead counters needed because rituals play no great role in the hard work of consciously activating, maintaining, and protecting the Kingdom. The call of scripture is for justice, for which ritual preoccupations are useless except as tools that prop the ever failing aegis of poseurs.

The divine ethics of operative freemasonry do not permit Machiavellian obfuscation unless at war. Strength and honor are manifest best when grace benefits all, individually and collectively. Contrition marks our conscious ascent to leadership, as wee decision makers who discern correctly, great and small, be it castle or hamlet. Its chair permits us to judge matters as divinely appointed agents. Repentance begins the ascent with abject death to the self-centered ambitions that plague all toddlers. Then comes the renaissance of latent inspiration to guide us to enact the *Will of God* after attaining skills and desire to do so during adolescence.

It is all too easy to get side-tracked and lose sight of this transcendental processing, that some call the development of *christos consciousness* that rebirths us *into* the world without being singularly focused on its matter because we now attend the continuum of unseen and seen realms. Because this is a genuine ascent into the moral reality of life after making the cut, it forbids the melodrama of the shadow's *stigmata*, which is purposely absent in Dali's "Last Supper". Thus, the gifted artist set his redeemed sacred heart in perfectly balanced ascendence, powered by the anti-gravity of reverent geometrical juxtapositions of all elements and participants; seen and unseen. From whence comes such symmetry?

While on earth, penitent humility repeatedly re-accesses the supernal grace our Adamic race seems to have lost. When joined to marital fidelity it opens even mightier portals that attract and procure more virile ethers in concert with dynamic processes that disperse reproductive radiance, initially as plasma photons. Life mysteriously respires at this sub-atomic interface, where *systems-mingling*s and *-couplings* occur when apposite fractals are aligned in resonant, *tensor-vibrational* harmonies that, in turn, affect beneficial outcomes before telomeres are charged to amass the first morula. When all such exchanges are held to be sacrosanct, something miraculous marks and follows that embryo for life. This sacrality is too often defiled by poseurs and rakes. It is what I and many failed men have done, including Mr Poole, whose penalties are especially doubled due to hypocrisy.

Without a sacralized focus, suffering and loss result for want of informed integration of knowledge with the wisdom of experience. Together they implement the divine protection afforded by supplemental grace. Secret Services mistakenly compensate for it by gathering furtive 'intelligence'. But spying is un-Islamic because it discounts intuitions gained from righteous intent during our pursuit of justice. Instead of G-d, we become dependent of spies, which is how Poole lived and exploited his Negroes. Hence, humanity blindly obtains harm more readily than benefit for want of rahim grace; and this, depending on knowledge levels, beliefs held, choices made, and deeds done. All begins with parents. Hence, when bad things happen to good or innocent people, such as vaccine and covid scams, or the firebombing(s) of Dresden, Vietnam, Laos, and Gaza, it is not G-d's fault. Such outcomes are built into existence as direct outcomes deriving from non-sacrosanct, human choices. It is a law of dis-grace.

Because faithfulness, and integrity attract, identify, and actuate suitably paired electromagnetic flux patterns and *EMF*-fractals at quantum levels, consider the possibility that lies and liars attract incorrect or poorly matched patterns and frequencies that fail to congruently complement the *other* half of an already distressed pair or morula. By default, nature's *yin-yang* laws obligingly correct or isolate insults to the sacred geometry of apposite pairing by responding in kind. Accordingly, as *little gods* we enhance life by forbidding poor pairings in favor of better informed choices. To the contrary, should we fail to ascend, we become *little devils* who cause harm by activating incorrectly informed or wickedly purposed, ungodly pairings, such as mRNA Covid-vaccine NSA-propaganda, or NOI's melanin-based rhetoric. All such errors forbid transcendent, Vitruvian symmetry (Chap 13).

the grace of divine kinship

Using this model, it becomes apparent that mountebanks like Poole damage life by altering, deterring, mismatching,

Contrition

or repressing beneficial *EMF* patterns established by The Great Mystery's *logos*. Those who enable liars like him assist the subversion of *logos* by default. They do this by activating an aspect of spiritual law that autonomously executes the obverse outcomes that invite nemesis. This happens when men abort destiny's straight and narrow path and opt for fate's wide road to hell.

For example, despite mountains of evidence to the contrary, current inversions of truth permit toxic insults while authorities promote them as beneficial. This capacity for abject dissociation from truth at grave costs to others overwhelms reason. It is what cross-dressers and narcissists typically do. Denial's administrators and agencies misuse prayer by failing to maintain operative synchronicity with The Great Mystery's *logos*. Instead, and by default, they synchronize neuro-political efforts* with organized evil. This is the *Mystery of Iniquity* in action. Some call it *poneros*.

Impure motives and intent short circuit, corrupt, and/or prevent us from accessing the beneficent sub-atomic dynamics of *rahim* grace. It is a process that has finally been described by Noetic Science:

> 🗝 WHAT HAS BEEN PROPOSED is that each molecule in the body sends out a unique electromagnetic field that can 'sense' the field of a complimentary molecule [reciprocity]. It's as if there is a 'dance' in the cellular medium and the molecules move to the vibratory rhythm. We note that music is also supplied by biophotons ...
>
> 🗝 about 100,000 chemical reactions happen in every cell each second. A chemical reaction can only happen if the molecules reacting are excited by a photon. Once the photon has excited a reaction, it returns to the field and is available for more reactions... [Thus], we are swimming

in an ocean of light ... [exactly as Tesla posited of the ether]

🔑 If you examine a neuron, you will see many hollow tubes surrounding the axon. These microtubules had previously been thought of as a kind of scaffold to support the nerve fiber. But they are now getting a second look at the possible architecture of our consciousness. The characteristics of microtubules that make them suitable for quantum effects include a crystal-like lattice structure, a hollow inner core, organized cell function, and capacity for information processing.

🔑 According to researchers, *their size appears perfectly designed to transmit photons in the UV range. This indicates a system of bio-fiber optics per intelligent design.* The microtubules cited have since been found throughout the fascia where discrete nexii and nodal points correspond with acupuncture meridians. Japanese scientists have called it the primo-vasuclar system

🔑 The primo vascular system has a specific anatomical and immuno-histochemical signature that sets it apart from the arteriovenous and lymphatic systems. With immune and endocrine functions, the primo vascular system has been found to play a large role in biological processes, including tissue regeneration, inflammation, and cancer metastases.

🔑 Although scientific studies confirmed in 2002, the original discovery was made in the early 1960s by Bong-Han Kim, a North Korean scientist. It would take nearly 40 years after that discovery for scientists to revisit Kim's research to confirm the early findings.

🔑The presence of primo vessels in and around blood and lymph vessels, nerves, viscera, and fascia, as well as in the brain and spinal cord, reveals a common link that could potentially open novel possibilities of integration with cranial, lymphatic, visceral, and fascial approaches in manual medicine.[4]

To the chagrin of monotheist imaginations, Noetic Science defines things that would have condemned us to the stake a few hundred years ago in Protestant or Catholic worlds. *The Dao*'s scientific wing can now measure various fractals, *EMF*s, and other vectors and outcomes to determine attributions concerning moral and immoral intent. Indeed, we can now forensically prove that people who resist truth are in a state-of-sin: the default sub-human setting of grace-forbidding, self-centered consciousness. Like Mr Poole, they cannot help but inform and affect the futile cyclosis of magical thinking. Similar to davening Semites and Parsees, they repeatedly dash hope by subverting revealed knowledge with superstition, and thus, like Pharisees and stubborn mullahs, prevent everyone under their sway from entering the kingdom (Matt.23:13).

Only clear waters of contrition can restore our ability to access and process the supernal grace that attends divine

---

4. **references**

Stefanov M, et al. (2013). The Primo Vascular System as a New Anatomical System. J Acupuncture & Meridian Series. 6(6):331-338; https://doi.org/10.1016/j.jams.2013.10.001

"Langevin HM and Yandow JA (2002). Relationship of acupuncture points and meridians to connective tissue planes. PUB MED: Anat Rec. 269(6):257-65, DOI: 10.1002/ar.10185"

* See: Qvortrup, M. (2024). The Political Brain: The Emergence of Neuropolitics. Central European University Press. https://doi.org/10.7829/jj.4032514 // and https://politicalscience.jhu.edu/faculty-books/neuropolitics-thinking-culture-speed/

also: Omar Zaid, Sexology For The Wise, p 21. https://forum.alginkgo.com/go/WT65DjLFk5

kinship. So, let us unpack the futile cyclosis of **NOI**'s unseen coin.

3

CHASTE EARTH
COVENANT CONDITIONS

good faith

This reiterative dialectic mimes scripture's mimesis. Of interest are syncretic parallels, histories, and doctrines found in numerous cults. I argue that the nidus of NOI failure is marital infidelity, which nigh universally and generously infects society in due form to arrest our peaceful evolution. Since Nature prefers quality reproductive seed (Matt.12.13), I further argue that the very best product of this divinely sourced complimentary pairing is homo-sapient offspring. Thus, all implications are hugely spiritual and material, which I view as a continuum or unity, as do all reasonably settled sojourners, but not in the monist sense.

In NOI's favor we note vital disciplines that forbid vulgar sensationalism and waste. However, in the scheme of things perennially intended for our good, even per dumb luck, these saplings have yet to be set in the enriched soil of a repentant nursery that holds-fast-to and exclusively protects truth fractals that are required for healthy reproduction. In keeping with the *New Physics* of Noetic Science, intuitive and other forms of energy both physically and psychically touch *The Great Mystery's* impenetrable *logos* for better or worse depending on intent and circumstance.[1] Moreover, after setting Hellenized and Judeo-Romanized interpolations aside, we note that *logos* is neither out of Africa, nor of Rome, nor *ex nililo*, nor of *Hesus* or *Bhraman* anthropomorphic fantasies.

The Son of Miriam, mistakenly called ~~Jesus~~, is like all of us, just another *word made flesh* with live drives and a job to do. Contrary to accretions and errant interpretations, scripture clearly says *logos* proceeds from some unfathomably ineffable mystery to represent G-d's creative word. It is then cryptically, intelligently, systematically, and supernally applied to 'things unseen' with a view to cause what is seen. King James generously rendered *'out of things unseen'* as *'out of nothing'* or *ex nihilo*. Others claim it is ~~Jesus~~ as G-d Himself, our suicided savior. Similar lies have been foisted on us from time-immemorial by extremely cunning confidence men, allowing fools to think they are exceptionally wise.

When unopposed by magical thinking, trans-dimensional fractal substrates reverberate with sub-atomic complementarities that penetrate our material world out of the cited 'unseen realms' to instruct, construct, and even reconstruct (heal) various components and processes that incarnate and preserve our genus as homo-*sapient*-sapiens. Proverbs 18.21 even says that *"Death and life are in the power of the tongue,"* or spoken word. Words not only reflect but also

---

1. SEE: **SEXOLOGY FOR THE WISE** : essays on marriage, queers, and occult governance; Vol II Marriage, Metaphysics and Genesis 501.1 https://forum.alginkgo.com/go/NTzOMIeg2i

help shape the reality of our relationships, attitudes, and spiritual lives. Hence:

> 🗝 if pristine fractals are to benefit existential patterns made subject to our co-creative tongue, then habits of knowledge acquisition married to morally-imbued skill sets are required to optimize outcomes.

Hence again,

> 🗝 we best learn to speak coherently and in congruence with G-d so as not to subvert unseen aspects of divine intent.

This purpose of prayer—what Muslims call *solat*—is to establish genuine *communication*s with the unseen so as to comprehend and then cooperate with *logos*: to communicate specifically with this intent in mind, full expecting a coherent response.

Ideally, covenants bind us to a sacred trust* such as the good faith that founded America as a Confederated Republic under G-d; which by convention meant 'national submission to our super-intelligent and ineffable Source Creator'. Such governance should yield fruits that hold suitably modified epigenetic qualities pursuant to repentance from deeds and thoughts that yield the self-centered outcomes of homo-*stupidus*, whom the bible calls "bad fruit", even "chaff". This is why informed Operative Freemasons like George Washington and his college of "*dangerous men*",* left dying Europe in opposition to Speculative Freemasonry's *Illuminati*.[2] Legatees of the latter circles

---

2. **TRUST: Ontogeny & Misplacement** Chapter III: 'Touch, Trust, &

have since turned American governance over to incorporated agencies in the service of a covert commercial empire or *hegemon*, owned by families of the Old World Order and their trusted satraps.

> * 🔎 Repair yourself to Taverns, Trading posts, stables and all public places. There you will enlist dangerous men in his Majesty's service under my Command. You shall meet me with your company in 12 days Saturday Rappahannock Royal Arsenal at the hour of bells. You shall arrive on the hour sharp and without excuses.

11/17/24_sms, JT Bard to Omar Zaid: From Major Commander George Washington, a missive to JT Bard's ancestor during the French and Indian War (1757). Private Library.

Renewing this husbandry obtains the lost garden of genuine human affairs. From an eschatological perspective, I believe it is our greatest challenge. If I am correct, then sapient co-creating seed-carriers are called on to address all disciplines with a view to optimize fractal usage under the consciously imbued facilitation of informed councils that view life as it is, moment-to-moment, while at the same time keeping pace with all current events and developments. Similar congresses should guide the pragmatic applications of knowledge synthesis for communal benefit.

Per Goethe, the cardinal analytical elements required

Deception' https://forum.alginkgo.com/go/8WkEa0Cp8Y Chapter II: "A Just Social Order"

Also **THE HAND OF IBLIS**, An Anatomy of Evil: The Hidden Hand Of The New World Order, Summary Observations and History https://forum.alginkgo.com/go/BdW6eMMbco

for such purposes include a recital of a phenomenon's complete narrative. Such an approach summarily rejects reductionism and 'special interests' because only a holistically-informed perspective can comprehensively establish archetypes comprised of fundamental fractals out of which beneficial developments that complete teleology proceed. If such is the case, and it seems so, then authentic contemplative meditations—in the rationally scientific sense—inherently oppose mindless iterations of word salads divorced from practical knowledge, which describes many religions and political theories devised by homo-*stupidus* replicants. This further suggests that a complete descriptive narrative must imbue informed councils with *Science, Scripture, and History*.

Some of us will eventually accomplish the commission, G-d willing, on and within planet earths already prepared, per eschatology; which indicates that our present *terra firma* is a place of winnowing, engineered to see who makes the cut. Hence, folks who uncritically honor the immanence of pseudo-deific eminences like Mr Poole are herein advised not to take celestially sourced fractals out of context or for granted. Moreover, if you seriously wish to make the cut, do not sow seed within walls that conceal rudely-placed desires.

who makes the cut

Scriptures variously indicate that we can and do become homo-*sapient* after yielding to the bitter winds of Moriah.[3] This painfully passionate process holds immanent judgment

---

3. for astute dissertation on Moriah, see Abarim Publications https://www.abarim-publications.com/

and necessarily precedes our re-gaining access-to the supernal grace that aids whatever ordeal is required for personal or communal re-ascendance. In honor of this moment of magic, Christians call it epiphany or '*Holy Spirit*', indicating an awakening to G-d consciousness or '*christ within*', so to speak. Nonetheless, there are myriads of messengers, messages, and *christs-within* that synchronously and everywhere whisper multi-lingual fractals of veridically holy import, moment-to-moment. Informed synchronicity and appropriate messaging is the problem because it requires complementary pairings at sub-atomic plasma levels of touch where the unseen forms the seen.[4]

Listening to the harmony of these spheres of etheric plasma requires great care; but obedience requires even graver attention (*gravitas*) to beneficial management systems we all too readily abandon to seriously-minded mountebanks like Mr Poole. Such persistent-predatory-personalities (PPP) assiduously resist and do their very best to circumvent justice by creating false narratives (myths) and protocols that undergird constitutions, religions, and laws for the sake of their favorite country club and barber shop. Post-Enlightenment *Corporate* and *Banking* laws especially represent this tide of evil.[5] PPPs and their lackeys are the bane of Billy Budds and Malcolm-Xs everywhere (see Chapter 7).

When we obey after receiving the message, by operative experience we quickly learn that inspired fractal enhancements are reserved for faithfully obedient servants of truth.

---

4. * See: **Touch, Trust, and the Case for Forensic Ponerology** https://forum.alginkgo.com/go/plrbZjEwlu
5. Alexander Del Mar https://forum.alginkgo.com/go/GIkXptPcOc https://forum.alginkgo.com/go/HGXbIZNi1e required reading for serious students.

Contrition

The experience sets them apart with an *in-the-world* but *not-of-it* attitude. Moreover, because one must qualify for this responsible state of conscious perception, it marks a noble meritocracy of peers whose purpose and skills run boldly towards destiny. But this is a race that contradicts the doctrine of unconditional love. Hence, the author postulates:

- 🗝 the most prudent and challenging institution that preserves and prospers gestalt fractal inspiration as a complete microcosmic archetype is monogamous heterosexual marriage.
- 🗝 humble adherence to principles that guide the properly gendered management of relational fractals are brought to the parsing table when one reverently approaches The Great Mystery in service to a legitimate marital covenant.[6]

Only then do we begin to learn how best to consciously save face before Judgement Day; i.e., how to sift, protect, sort, plant, harvest and process good seed in chaste soil. This is genuine *communion*. Its time consuming process allows us to become discerning *sons* and *daughters* of maturity (*little gods*, meaning *lesser* decision makers). There are ranks. Allegorically this indicates polities that are faithful to the righteous ancestors to whom they are gathered after death, meaning inspired prophets and prophetesses (e.g.

---

6. * ***Sexology For The Wis**e* op.cit. https://forum.alginkgo.com/go/WT65DjLFk5
   ** ***Your Closest Neighbor***: A Manual For The Rightly Guided https://forum.alginkgo.com/go/bujAsmzXE9

White Buffalo Woman). I am of the opinion that the latter group of peers included Neanderthal types some 60-70,000 years ago, or more. Must have been folks like ole Abraham, Odin and Khrishna, or Miriam and her son, or Deborah. G-d knows who else. We don't. [7]

unholy ground

Parents begin this process naturally when unmolested by religious impositions. Priests pretend the estate but generally fail to slay its Medusa by decapitating the sin of pride. The conundrum faced is catholic because the *Kingdom of God* does not manifest in unchaste earth (clay). If I am correct, what leaders like Mr. Poole incarnate is their own palatinate, nefariously referred to in scripture as *Kings of the Earth*. Good Books also call clandestine bed-hoppers like him 'infertile soil' or unholy ground (impure clay). Although lauding chastity and fidelity, *Fard and Poole Ltd.* never taught the fullness of heaven's chaste earth policy as described herein because they were practitioners-of libidinous, male chauvinism.

By '*chaste earth*' I mean sexual lust reserved for the monogamous marriage (union) of clay vessels we call *bodies* but which scripture calls *temples* for our souls. In no way does heaven expect its representatives on earth to be abstemious anchorites; although some who lack self-control obscenely self-castrate to prevent sexual sin out of extreme desperation. Ergo, the writer posits that monogamous

---

7. ***TRINITY: The Metamorphosis of Myth***: https://forum.alginkgo.com/go/5zVvL07vLe

conjugal chastity is the missing cornerstone of NOI's edifice (1.Pet.2.4).

Carnal hypocrisy rests uneasily in hyper-vigilant hearts. I experienced the neurosis as a libertine doctor while noting that most of my patients also lied about sex, especially puritans. In NOI's case, the origin of this amply apologized-for perfidy lay with the enthusiastic permissiveness of Mirza Ahmadiyya's clan: a minority Muslim cult out of 19th Century Pakistan that apparently inspired Fard's adventures in American ghettos.

Ahmadiyya's cadre is filled to the brim with hagiographic Lotharios who lavishly preach fascinating *cul-de-sac* doctrines that proliferate hero worship.[8] With Stalinist ardor they imbue minions who, in turn, set about to ruin traditional High Culture(s) with the same imperious zealotry that politely sells girl scout cookies for Jesuits (see Appendices: Annunaki). They are similar to folks who persuade Muslims to kiss the Kaaba's black-stoned *Vulva de al' Lat* . I suspect the complacent smooching sacred stones, portraits, and rings that honor lies and liars is unholy ground that cannot host chaste earth or rahim grace.

But there is hope.

4

GOLGOTHA
THE MYSTERY OF SALVATION

Dalí believed that the seemingly separate and incompatible concepts of science and religion can in fact coexist.

the christos path

REPENTANCE UNBARS the *christos* path; which is the transcendent elevation of mundane awareness to degrees of responsible mindfulness for everlasting consequences, whereby truth sets us relatively free from lies and liars. It ain't ~~Jesus~~ but it is what the son-of-Miriam did. This 'dao-within' instructs us to die to selfishness, which, in turn, mercifully allows our vigilant reunification with supernal, pre-elemental fractals brimming with divine grace and will. On certification we continually hear, recite, and act out the following invocation: *"Not mine but thy will be done"*—in stark opposition to initiations that bear the Luciferian, '*do what thou wilt*' motto.

As requisite credentials before entering the noble ranks of leadership —which is Tolkein's *Elvin* Domain— operational acolytes analogously pass through Blue Lodges at the bottom-three rungs of Jacob's pyramidal ladder'—through apprentice, journeyman, and master degrees. Each grade teaches us to better control our melodramatic whims so that temperament gives way to informed reason. Even so, such steps are primitive compared to the degrees of knowledge and skill required for community leadership. Those ranks require skill sets that admit the successful completion of parent- and spouse-hood as requisite experience;[1] which is why adults without kids become uncomfortably sensitive. They know they are unqualified.

Since communal welfare should never be placed in unqualified hands, this principle disqualifies parents of reprobates as well as folks under the fifth decade of life, regardless of intellectual or professional accomplishments. After completing all three degrees, by the fifth decade a person't trustworthy competence as a sapient elder is well underway. Parenthood and marital fidelity each hold narra-

---

1. **YOUR CLOSEST NEIGHBOR**, The Seven Basic Needs Of Your Spouse https://forum.alginkgo.com/go/dU5d6AS647

that boast honorable achievements. Both Fard and Poole failed in these regards.

Whereas, in prophet Mohammad's case, we have Khadijah bint Khuwaylid, to whom he was monogamously married for twenty-five years; and Fatima, their well-married daughter. Claims that Mohammad had multiple wives appear to be bogus interpretations (see Appendices, *On Polygamy*).* The NOI parallel is this: just as the right honorable Malcolm-X exposed the adultery of his mentor, so did Mohammad condemn idolatry and establish a model for individual and confederate governance that has since been abandoned.

> *The right honorable Sister Khadijah was a Hanif Christian who considered Iesa, the Son of Miriam, a prophet, not God.* [2]

the real blue lodge

1. *bachelor's degree* (= qualified for marriage) after completing **Apprenticeship**; i.e., childhood, latency, and adolescence (7 years each)

2. *marriage* (OJT work experience) —providing one is eligible— this earns a ***Journeyman's*** degree.
   - It's a kind-of middle school leading to middle age that includes mating, and nest-and-family building while keeping all three

---

2. SEE: Ibn Ishaq, **The Life of Muhammad**, Alfred Guillaume (trans.) Oxford University Press, 1979. https://forum.alginkgo.com/go/vNr2KaNGGw

in order along with responsibly meeting community standards.

3. The successful and collective *raising of children* during this period grants a **Masters Degree** along the way. It's a combined program.
   - Except for the captaincy of small or regional collectives, this degree offers adjutant-level only appointments, as all positions are held directly accountable to advanced degree holders who have successfully submitted their PhD thesis.

4. **Successful PhD Candidates** prove their own and their children's fruit good with congruent narratives. This takes them from Grey to White Sage *Sagan* status and ends mid-life.
   - ***the doctoral Sage*** (Sagen)**:** at 60 years or thereabouts, one become eligible for advanced degrees in kingdom leadership that concerns the well-being of a confederacy of collectives (think *Medina*).

One now appreciates how far off-course we are under the captaincy of Speculative Freemasonry; you know, folks who put Macrons and Trudeaus in seats of power. Indigenous societies naturally mark the developmental steps just cited as degrees of maturity. It is why white haired elders are held in such high regard. In fact, many oriental societies would not suffer the disgrace of old folks homes.

A person's reputation as trustworthy or not is, therefore and generally speaking, established by their fifth decade of life, which is the beginning of midlife. This is the archetypal template for the firmest of foundations upon which Divinely Ordered Institutions are fashioned by sapient humans. If one remains unqualified, submission to those who do qualify is the only peaceful solution; which challenge courts humility, because it is what committed spouses do for each other. As the reader will soon appreciate from a scientific perspective, arguments to the contrary inhibit the due ordering of sacred geometry.

The Great Mystery deems contrition and fidelity necessary to access fluent streams of divine guidance *before* handing the reigns of revision to qualified leaders (Q.4.17-18). Since experience is operative initiation, it is appreciably greater than imaginary epiphanies or hagiographic apotheosis as pretended by celibates like Ignatius Loyola. Pretenders and their minions often regale gilded evangelical mandarins with kissable stones, bones, genitalia, sacred wood, and fanciful imaginations such as Mr Poole's spaceship on the dark side of the moon.

Thus it is wisdom and skill gained by experience that erects the edifice of fidelity on a firm foundation of truth and justice. Building this temple, this son-of-man-Adam, is the goal of Operative Freemasonry. Unbeknownst to pedestrians who've been conditioned by Speculative Freemasons or their agents; operatives who remain deign to build body and soul as a *living temple* dedicated to reverent contemplation with a view to effectively plan and act in good faith (*bonafide*) for the good of all, most especially for helpless women and children. Hence, Dali's transcendence is *christos* salvation. St Peter made this operative focus perfectly clear:

> 🗝 ***You yourselves, like living stones***
> are being built up as a spiritual house, to
> be a holy priesthood, to offer spiritual

sacrifices *[good deeds]* acceptable to God through *christos ascendence* (1 Peter, 2.5)

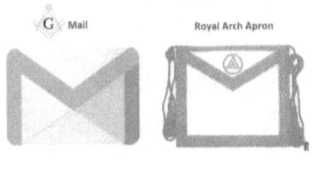

conventional villainy

Prince Hall Lodges reverberate with the same Orientalist thematics that guide every Proto-Indo-Iranian-Ayran lodge, all of which are Semite challenged, east and west of the Volga. These tenets played a significant role in NOI's genesis and pedagogy.* Despite ribbons of ostensible ethics, they lack genuine operative facility for kingdom policies because they are an amalgam of truth minced with generous dollops of fancy that can only be used to erect a roguish edifice on unsound foundations.

This indictment applies to all who flaunt the aprons and layers of speculative deceptions proffered by modern and post-modern Luciferians on the square. Most of their degrees were surreptitiously added by Jacobin and Jacobite agents (i.e., Kabbalist Jews and Jesuits) post 1717 CE.** Thus, thirty-three degrees of conventional villainy on both sides of any aisle stand between the deep state of Google's apron and heaven's decree; notwithstanding the Washington Monument's phallic imposition on behalf of Madams Isis and Rothschild.***

> * 🗝 Freemasonry's upper degrees, post-Blue Lodge, command loyalty to Zionism per Talmud and Kabbalah precepts.[3]

---

3. ** Cain's Creed, The Cult(s) of Rome. https://forum.alginkgo.com/go/rS-iVukcgS

*** 🗝 Jesus and James were master architects and engineers according to Roman soldiers who left an oral tradition (Equestrians) backed by documents commonly ignored by mainstream theologians.

> Source: JT Bard, *operative poet*,
> alginkgo.com

The personal knowing of spiritual and material science comprises the *gnosis* of Operative Freemasonry. Its seat is the rock upon which Moses and Joshua found *Al' Khidr* sitting like Rodin's *Thinker*. Abstract speculation, on the other hand, is neither knowledge nor experience but rather schoolboy playacting. However, even this or Mr Farrakhan's esteem for the CIA's Scientology psyop are insufficiently deplorable condemnations.

As cited previously, investigators vigorously suggest that not a few **NOI** platform planks were harvested from the same forests that subverted Islam with fabricated hadith. Substantial evidence also links **NOI** founders to the corrupt Theosophy of Madams Blavatsky and Besant, who both announced the return of Jesus a century ago. These and other repositories of guile stem from debased Zoroastrians, Ismailis, Nizaris, and Manichaeans, all hailing from the same magi lands that bred Kurdish and Talmud-loving Rabbins, crypto and not. Fifteen hundred years of *captive* and *post-captive* Yiddish evolution in Babylon at length birthed Khazarian Jewry's plague on Russia, Germany, the Ukraine, and now the globe.

🗝 *They were followers of Manichaeism*, who sponsored the Qur'an's Translation under the Abbasid Caliph, al-Mansur. They

Contrition

formed a committee of Syriac-speaking Christians and Persian speaking Zoroastrian Manichaeans.

🔎 *Mani was a Jew who converted to Christianity then founded his own sect, claiming his disciples were the 'Seal of the Prophets'. This literary effort expressed Manichaean doctrines and rituals, the superiority of Persian art and culture, and canonized Parsi as the inspired language of occult Islam. Hence, they brought Manichaeism into Islamic literature.* [4]

🔎 Fazlur Rahman convincingly reveals that many hadith, even among those considered reliable', are corrupted by a political bias that attempted to create a middle Islam' with the so-called 'orthodox' (Sunni) perspective in ascendency. As such, *the entire field of hadith research and subsequent application should be re-evaluated in light of his observation.* [5]

elevated negritude

NOI's hoary speculations elevated negritude with the same finesse Persian magi used to birth messianic Christian pretense—not to mention the Mahdi delusion of Alawite, Qadiani, cum Ahmadiyyah genesis; the latter being the most likely vessel for NOI accretions.

i. 🔎 We also believe that Elijah Poole was an ex-Qadiani (an indigenous sheikh) from the Mufti Muhammad Sadiq era (1920-1923). There were many of these.

~~ii.~~

---

4. * Dr Kasif Khan https://www.linkedin.com/pulse/translation-whole-quran-dr-kashif-khan
5. See: *Hadith and Sunnah-Ideals and Realities*, compiled and edited by P.K. Koya, Islamic Book Trust, KL, 1996.

- Elijah Poole mixed Ahmadiyya views with Alawite Shia beliefs and invented the Nation of Islam after Wallace Fard left in 1933.
iii. Furthermore, we believe that Eiljah Poole began lying about who Wallace Fard was, and also lied about him being Maulana Muhammad Abdullah (a Lahori-Ahmadi).
iv. Finally, we see all FBI reports on Wallace Fard as lies and concocted paperwork.
v. However, I must mention that my research work is incomplete, since we don't have copies of the *"Al-Bayan"* Arabic newspaper or the archives of the *Final Call* newspaper. [6]

Sundry Amorite adjuncts dealing with astro-theology were added during the early development of this astro-religio-neuro-political scheme when it held Nimrod's chairs at Sargon the Great's University of Sippara.* By the time of ~~Jesus~~, the Sephardi Exarch dominated most of Jewry, including Jerusalem. Even prior to Europe's Enlightenment, subtle Judeo-friendly myths and *egregore* had neo-conned many thrones. By the Time of Bismark, Hidden Masters had sedulously usurped and misguided all worshipful chairs of every lodge by unabashedly honoring Zionist supremacy with new degrees in windowless rooms behind closed doors that mattered the most.

After Alexander's fallen star they added Elysian to Mithraic mysteries, all of which blithely modified even more hoary legacies. Scholars politely call these accretions *Hellenization*. Two thousand years later, midway through the

---

6. My book review of Dr. John Andrew Morrow's,"Finding W.D. Fard: Unveiling the Identity of the Founder of the Nation of Islam"

18th Century AD, *The Council of the Emperors of the East and West*—Jewish Magi of *The Rite Of Perfection*—[7] determined *i*) to usurp Speculative Freemasonry, as well as *ii*) occupy chief chairs at all colleges, and *iii*) marry into every noble house of Europe's fallen equestrians. This dear friends is neither transcendence nor elevated negritude. But it is the Mystery of Iniquity's political science in action

* NB: Zoroastrianism a legitimate monotheist repository of wisdom.

---

7. See: **The Hand of Iblis**, pp 294-295 https://forum.alginkgo.com/go/uxr7aWYRBF and my Campfire Talks on Freemasonry and The Great Divide https://forum.alginkgo.com/go/LgjAm9fO6t

5

ILLUMINES
PROTOCOLS FOR CAIN'S CREED

🔎 *The Illuminés have initiates all over Europe, that they have spared no effort to introduce their principles into the [Masonic] lodges, and to spread a doctrine subversive of all settled government ...*
🔎 *Under the pretext of the regeneration of social morality and the amelioration of the lot and condition of men by means of laws founded on principles and sentiments unknown hitherto and contained only in the heads of their leaders.*

Francois Charles de Berckheim

Special Commissioner of Police, Mayence (Mainz, 1813) 1

---

1. Official Report written by Francois Charles de Berckheim, Special Commissioner of Police, Mayence (Mainz, 1813). Excerpt from ***Trust: Ontogeny and Misplacement*** https://forum.alginkgo.com/go/8WkEa0Cp8Y

Contrition

mummy dust

AND THAT'S WHAT IT IS: *sentiments unknown* to the sound forensic reasoning that keeps us on the straight and narrow. Aristotle repented of handing this mummy dust to Iskandar. He fully intended to go public with Alexander's godman farce—all of it even then imbued with much of what's become modern Masonic garbage. Indeed, I'm sure Aristotle caused the murderously beligerent lad to seethe with homicidal rancor. Indeed, capital punishment for treason is traditionally imposed on gang members who rat-out apostles of cultural subversion. In terms of a typical nondisclosure agreement, it no doubt eased the skids for those who marshaled Malcolm's shot-gun assassination from across the river.

Scripture presents this archetype as the execution of Pharaoh's repentant magi. Brother Malcolm was in the throes of similar contrition when they cut him down like a dog. He discarded NOI's cultured magick and would no longer stand as Poole's chamberlain to incessantly bellow *anti-logos* in defiance of *christos* flux. He would no longer be casting for the mental colonization of *gog's* challenge to all who become *magog*. But semite vanity finds no rest in Judaized negritos after barbershop falsifications multiply. Already drunk on mundane injustice, with a newly acquired stupor they managed a utopian sway of hysteria for their messiah. As commissars of the dead, NOI boasted and feasted on the magnificent rot of intoxicating impostures that held festering buboes, *lettres de cachet le Harut & Marut*.

In eschatological terms, not just NOI but the entire world has been neo-conned by British Zionists, a legacy that began in earnest with professors *Harut & Marut* in Babylon (Q.2.102). They apparently tagged and taught *Gog* fraternities and sororities how to be successful moon-worshipping leaders of insignificant light—that is, *gog elitists* of compoundedly ignorant followers called *magog*.* This is post-grad Political Science 502; 501 being the sun-worship of Ancient Babil & Sumer's astro-theology.

As a paraphrased synopsis that draws on remarks made by several observers, I offer the following profile to help put this in perspective:

> 🗝 Al'Qur'an suggests that Harut & Marut were well-informed elders at Siparra University who revised esoteric and exoteric religions with a view to imbued them with specific chauvinist accretions for the purpose of legitimizing imperial plunder under elitist auspice.

> 🗝 Put simply, they were the Round Table CFR of the day whose institute taught initiatory protocols for Cain's Creed, *and whose* DP-*tentacles assured bureaucratic compliance with neuro-political subservience.*

Similar planks are still noised abroad as para-scriptural literature** that misguides globally. Generally, these traditions ignore or stretch the allegorical and metaphorical verity of inspired knowledge. We find apologists with kissable rings and stones everywhere routinely mincing truth with customary lies to increase bottom lines, harems, temple bling, and ballot boxes. As Jesuit pedants duly note, the blind following of lies is readily achieved within three-to-four generations after the death of legitimate reformers.

This is the time it takes for G-d to prepare a sage and is not news for informed historians.

* 🔑 **Gog & Magog:** sometimes referred to as territories north of Syria, including Russia (Rosh), from which hail Slavs and Aryans: i.e. Gog and Magog, respectively ... or Shamhazai and Azael, or Iannes and Iambres. Ashkenazie Jews are predominantly east European Slavs. This god's most ancient symbol is the Crescent Moon, held in common with the moon god named *Sin*. Harut and Marut were two idols worshipped in ancient Armenia. A writer from those regions speaks of them in the following passage:

__ Certainly Horot and Morot were tutelary deities of mount Ararat. There is a Sanskrit story of the similar ascent of two angels, and a Houri like Zohra, from which Armenians may possibly have taken their tale. From this idolatrous source Jews no doubt received it; and from them, the Moslems.

__ **The word *giant* was misconstrued** to signify not those who tyrannically "fell" on the poor people around them, but to angels who "came down, or fell, from heaven. NB: the term used is **Nefilim**, which simply means *'persons who fell upon the helpless around them and committed violence and oppression on earth.'* [plunderers]

** 🔑 Men who withstand the truth using myths and fairytales are corrupt in mind and reprobate concerning the faith ... From the *Gospel of Nicodemus* we learn they were **sorcerers**. ... Harut and Marut ... The charge brought against Jews is that when the Book of Allah was put before them they pretended not to recognize it, and instead resorted to the use of **spells taught by Harut and Marut**

> I suspect these are the spells of RELIGIO-NEURO-POLITICAL PROPAGANDA?
> ~ oz

*** 🗝 The figure of antichrist in Judaism, though based in part on the *gog* of Ezekiel and the *fourth beast* in Daniel, only makes his fully developed appearance in the Jewish Apocrypha. This tradition is closely paralleled by the Shiïte Muslim story that when the Mahdi comes he will be defeated and killed by the Antichrist, after which the Antichrist himself will be slain by the prophet Jesus.

references 2

hoodwinked pilgrims

NOI disciples received this mummy dust only to mime the worship of god-men saviors found the world over, including my once unrepentant, christian self. Sadly, poorly-informed and purposely-misdirected Blue Lodge acolytes are but hoodwinked pilgrims who often salute a pathocracy that happily leads their self-sacrificing hearts to ruin. They comprise a franchise of soporific empaths who have been deceived into thinking they are *knowers*. Thus do the spiritually dead of favored arcana advance the way of

---

2. * SEE: W. St. Clair-Tisdall, The Sources of Islam https://www.goodreads.com/book/show/20444668-the-sources-of-islam

** D. S. Magoliouth, Oxford, The Muslim World, Vol. XX, 1930, pp. https://www.answering-islam.org/Books/Margoliouth/harut_marut.htm

*** Charles Upton (2004). Legends of the End

Also: THE HAND OF IBLIS, An Anatomy of Evil: The Hidden Hand Of The New World Order, Summary Observations and History https://forum.alginkgo.com/go/uxr7aWYRBF

compounded ignorance to permit chemtrails, toxic metals, 5G weaponization, nano-carbon, and C-19-mRNA to enter the bloodstreams and fractals of their loved ones. It is why Brother Malcolm warned us not to let them educate our children.

We now know that hoodwinking spellbinders are persistant predators who use mummy dust to do the following:

🔎 **They clearly collude with each other and work in clusters** [gangs] ... they somehow recognize the predator in each other, or are influenced by each other in some way, and operate in rings, meanwhile carrying on all this holier than thou behavior, conducting prayers, weddings, funerals, and baptisms. It's unbelievable.

🔎 All non-forensic practitioners said **they are sadistic**, as did 88% of forensic practitioners. ... They are **above the law**. My experience showed their own self-interest was the only law.

🔎 This research indicates that ... including predators who are higher functioning such as those working in the fields of religion, law, academia, medicine, business and teaching, **they have no boundaries** or respect for the law, moral codes, or agreements **as they pertain to sexuality and/or relationships**.

🔎 The core driver of this **petty tyranny** in organizations occurs when one 'lords his or her power over others'. She cites another researcher who considers coercive control "*a liberty crime that erodes personal freedoms and choice, resulting in* **subjugation of the victim**."

🔎 In cults, this egotism takes a form "whereby their truth is the absolute and only truth, and no opposing view is tolerated.

🔎 The data indicate that great attention is often directed towards minimizing exposure. Considerable planning and time may be invested in creating opportunities for COVERT SEXUAL EXPRESSION, including the creation of 'false lives' that serve as covers to hide behaviors. ***They attack those who expose them or blame their victims***.

David Abramovitz:

a. They shunt away evidence to the contrary while proudly and militantly wearing pathocratic garments that mark an infantile resistance to truth.

b. This defiant petulance is a toddler's quandary that belies a complete lack of self-trust, which translates as paranoia, which root is an incomplete human identity marked by discernible boundaries;

c. They lack insight because they cannot learn from experience. (see appendices for more)

Elijah Poole ticks most of the above boxes.

Because identity confirmation for kingdom leadership requires a chaste marriage credential, betrayal is expected when dealing with any *DP* persona. For them, criminal infidelity is innate because their entire epigenetic input is enmeshed with the ponerogenesis of crossed interpersonal boundaries.

REFERENCES[3]

Bearing in mind that *Speculative* rather than *Operative* Freemasonry constructed the global network that presently unveils our eschatological imaginations of *Gog* and *Magog* (see: J Harland),[4] I pray the reader better appreciates how compounded ignorance serves those who organize the evils espoused by The Mystery of Iniquity for the Amorite hordes of gog and magog who about to bring it to completion.

Pro patria speculation ruins seed bearers with *pseudo*-fractals that stifle transcendence and reason with the magical thinking of hagiographic hero worship. Ultimately, this semiotic Humanism supports god-man idolatry (e.g. ~~Jesus~~) by forbidding a more comprehensive cosmological perspective that would mold us into sustainably trustworthy souls whose relationships could stand the test of time without genocidal mania. One path leads to hell, the other to

---

3. SEE: *Studying the Psychopath: Bones of Contention*. Harrison Koehli, Ponerology, 90 Aug 2024. https://forum.alginkgo.com/go/sWPkEfVTzD

and Anita Teresa. Remedies for Narcissism, Sadism & Masochism. https://forum.alginkgo.com/go/466UKFSzDo

related works:

Sacred Sadism, Gaia's Cord & The New Matriarchy THE ECO-FETISHIST ART OF GENEVIEVE BELLEVEAU https://forum.alginkgo.com/go/IkHtZUNrdf

M F Cusak (1896). The Black Pope: A History of the Jesuits https://forum.alginkgo.com/go/eohZ5TXQw9

4. * Jessica L Harland-Jacobs (2007). **Builders of Empire: Freemasons and British Imperialism**, 1717-1927. ~ https://uncpress.org/book/9781469613482/builders-of-empire/

success for humble sojourners. *Illumines* are on the poorly lit path of protocols for Cain's Creed.

Skeleton of a Puffer Fish
showing undisturbed fractals
in alignment with *kun-fia-kun / logos*

6

THE KINGDOM
ENTITLEMENT

kinship

SONS AND DAUGHTERS OF G-d abound in Judeo-Christian scriptures, and since Al Qur'an says G-d teaches pretty much the same things to all prophets (Q.41.42), I treat purity, both figuratively and literally, as the conjugal chastity that preserves trust in good faith with pure intentions, so that all social applications preserve family, clan, and nation to the exclusion of treasonous intent.

Literal and spiritual adultery, on the other hand, diverts or aborts the grace that naturally obtains the communal cohesion of like-minded kinship, which is the group-feeling gangs desire but rarely attain. Because adultery successfully subverts institutional integrity at all levels, it must be off-set by rituals that preserve the pretense of devotional loyalty. This allows politically-correct brides (polities) to stand by disloyal husbands with stern *gravitas*, even to the point of sutee. It is why Billy Budds and infants are sacrificed the world over for *pro patria* purposes. This misplaced-loyalty conundrum stands as NOI's dilemma. It is compromising Masonic gang initiation protocol for Blue Lodge minions who pledge allegiance.

🔑 In stark contradistinction I propose that loyalty to an exclusive coitus contract is what optimizes the institutionalization of moral and spiritual purity.

NOI's artifice thus plagues its own fabricated cultural identity template as a living parody; its double jeopardy gains trivial pleasures at the cost of moral, spiritual, and fully-informed emotional developments. Legatees assist the farce by misusing the term 'honorable', which compounds their misplacement of faith, hope, and trust in proven infidels.

When properly constituted and honored, marriage is the primal institutional fractal-processor supreme that guarantees lucid social cohesion; but only on condition that participants consider heterosexual conjugal chastity the most honorable of trustworthy human relations. This valuation redeems civilization by refracting divine aspirations at the apogee of submission to our indelible joinery with divine will. Its heartfelt devotional loyalty attracts and applies inexhaustible torrents of cosmic fractals (heavenly riches) that, when properly processed, help us avoid the mundane calamities that plague far too many.

Considering this and other arguments, I propose that marital fidelity is the microcosmic path to our becoming the *'little gods'* or *'judges'* mentioned in the Bible. This is to say, peacemaking adjutants who maintain social accords by doing our very best to ensure justice, beginning with self, spouse, and offspring. After judging correctly and over time, initiatory circumstances permit us to become praetorian mediators of justice—the other-worldly *Elves* of Tolkien's trilogy. Nobles like ~~Jesus~~, who men have stupidly deified, are spiritually related kin who naturally ally with anyone who is fiercely and gracefully armed with discernment per the ever-immanent divine guidance that attends reverent coitus and its memory. Notwithstanding the Wakanda fantasy, NOI's founders claimed this estate but made little progress in achieving its beatitude status (Q.21.92).

In *Sexology For The Wise* * I claim that chaste marital fidelity obtains a couple's consciously shared vision of Jacob's Ladder; referring to initiation into the *Dao* of divine order. It matters not what you call it, but well-matched couples consider its shared hope a path of near paradisiacal comfort not otherwise obtainable.* Marriage naturally follows its baccalaureate honeymoon with ongoing re-creative processes that birth degrees of graduate and post-graduate transfigurations as described previously. Its holy grail of transformative power best expresses satisfied fulfillment when:

i. 🗝 <u>wills are united:</u> un-compromising unity leads to the penultimate consummation of conjugal integrity (Q.21.92)
ii. 🗝 <u>this assures satisfaction:</u> faithful pairing attracts and actively maintains
iii. 🗝 supernal grace: <u>specifically allotted for them</u> to the exclusion of all others. [1]

Meeting and maintaining this level of satiation is the

---

1. See: https://forum.alginkgo.com/go/NTzOMIeg2i *Also: Your Closest Neighbor*: A Marriage Manuel https://forum.alginkgo.com/go/2VzHog7xVJ

Contrition

life-driving goal of our Hungry Ghost (Chapter 12). Communion at this level of consciousness peaks after keeping the following commandments:

🗝 **FIDELITY**: do not worship strange gods with another partner;

🗝 **EXCHANGE**: learn by the mutual experience of submitting-to and fulfilling each other's needs,

🗝 avoid the curse of fatalism by pursuing a jointly held vision of purpose that qualifies destiny, wherein **SHARED VISIONS** of faith, hope, and trust then manifest as testimony on a continuum (narrative).

🗝 should destiny's goodness give way to fatalism's narrative of weighty harm, something is surely amiss. Failing efforts at re-education and restoration, it is best to **DIVORCE IN PEACE** rather than pursue furtive relations or nurse what is cursed.

Conjugal fidelity's initiatory experiences are requisite benchmarks on a well-travelled road to wisdom. Hence, if you cannot complete the journey for whatever reason — and there are many— it is wise to humbly place your self and resources in the service of those who do so within the hierarchy of communal governance. Indeed, this is scriptural template for the kinship of Divinely Guided politics.

NOI congregants expected this auspice and most everyone who merits the nuptial franchise of coital fidelity at least glimpses the promise of its potential fruits. But be warned: if one never enters a legitimate bridal chamber, know that all imaginations and facsimiles so far fashioned fall short of an experience that should, much like The Great Mystery, never be mocked.

i. 🗝 In support of this assertion, scripture variously calls redeemed humans G-d's relatives or close kin with the utmost regard for legitimate marital relations.
    - ▶ Hence, a woman married to a Man-*of*-G-d symbolically represented G-d's spouse and vice versa.
    - ▶ In Christian terms, this refers to a communion of obedient disciples or *Body of Christ*, with Prophet Isa as head.

The satisfied countenance of such a couple's narrative during their fifth to eighth decades of life, especially after bearing the initial fruits of divine order, is all anyone ever really needs to know.

dp-narcissists

MARGARET MEAD wrote for the exclusively Jewish *Frankfurt School of Cultural Subversion* in support of LGBT-friendly ethics. This is not coincidental happens-chance. Promiscuous standards and cadre are foreign to *logos*. In no way are they inextricably woven into human existence as equal or preferred to the self-possessed morals of heterosexual fidelity.[2] Even so, clans of the uncoupled and uncouplelable avidly apologize for unrestrained lust; especially

---

2. * See ***Sexology***: "Playgrounds For The Uncoupled" https://forum.alginkgo.com/go/NTzOMIeg2i

J.D. Unwin & Why Sexual Morality May be Far More Important than You Ever Thought https://forum.alginkgo.com/go/dpDCMhR13s

that of politically-correct, self-centered, anti-social aspirations in stark opposition to optimized Divine Order.

Self-centered predators introduced in Chapter Five proliferate at institutions of governance that are often piloted by psycho-sociopath narcissists who dissociate sufficiently to rise above common sea levels as honored scum. Generally, Dark Personality (*DP*) narcissists exhibit a profile with the following traits:

- 🗝 are of higher intelligence and socioeconomic status;
- 🗝 have better impulse control;
- 🗝 are more adept at creating compelling facades;
- 🗝 engage more effectively in underhanded tactics that prevent exposure and accountability;
- 🗝 are better at grooming or manipulating others to support them;
- 🗝 are more likely to harm using methods that are subtle, ongoing, and leave no evidence, resulting in emotional and mental 'torture' which their targets/victims struggle to recount to others;
- 🗝 lead double lives.
- 🗝 **[Sadists]** have a cold-blooded sense of entitlement:
    - 🔎 all cult members are but parts to be moved around and utilized ... the perpetrator enjoys causing harm to multiple others yet poses as a heroic 'Jedi knight' to justify their actions in the guise of 'fighting evil' ... their entire public personality is a

construct: they use aliases to harm and hide wrongdoing. [3]

rivendale

In our search for a cure or preventative, we found a substantial corollary in Professor Unwin's systematic review of history a century ago.

> 🗝 Unwin found that when strict prenuptial chastity was abandoned, absolute monogamy, deism, and rational thinking disappeared within three generations. He also predicted the abandonment of rationalism, deism, absolute monogamy, and the collapse of western civilization in the third generation. [4]

Prurience becomes ubiquitous when we fail to curtail behaviors that advance the selfish violation of others. Our historical record indicates that chaste monogamy and premarital abstinence are incomparable tools of governance that yield lifetimes of meaningful and fulfilling relationships. Even so, we note that after violating others *DP*-perpetrators avoid shame, remorse, and restitution at all costs. What's more is their pugnacity reveals the arrested development of a defiant toddler. whose mutiny serves the whims of impure fractal processing. I'm guessing that not a few of these have passed their measured time for repentance (Q.20.129). Failing contrition, they often adopt apologetic

---

3. Psychopaths: Control through Calculated Ferocity
4. See: **Why Sexual Morality May be Far More Important Than You Ever Thought**, Kirk Durston / kirkdurston.com / 03 Dec 2019

myths that qualify entire nations for reprobation (Q.21.95-96).

Pretense arrests development so that the soul cannot transcend (mature) without the embodiment of moral virtue. Mr Tolkien kindly taught us that all responsible leaders must relinquish the rings of toddler power to attain Rivendale status. Only Elves and their guests can safely cross those fearsome waters. Only they gain access to portals of supernal grace by way of sapient humility. Indeed, genuine nobles are sojourners who turn aside to consider Noetic Science and *the Decalogue* of Moses, to which the son of Miriam recalled his nation. But Jews refused Al'Kitab in favor of Al' Talmud and Al' Kabballah.[5]

Fard & Poole Ltd.'s politically-correct institution carried the Malthusian burden by supersizing racial tension under chauvinist auspice. Ike Clanton did something similar in Tombstone when leading the Cowboy Gang. NOI became a conduit for minor and major iniquities in the wake of canted missionary zeal stoked by the promise of a jealous revenge against America's stale white crackers. His mild-mannered trance-making obtained ventriloquist pawns who cast a widening net of star-and-crescent fez-topped spell-binders on un-redeemable street corners where lesser evils grant the very least of *G-d's* mercies.

To the contrary, Mohammad judged a Confederacy in Medina where he was no shah of exceptional sociopaths who conquered others just to keep up with the Khans. To the contrary, he climbed through Blue Lodge degrees to successfully access rahim grace by seeking and keeping

---

5. SEE: **FORGOTTEN SAINTS** https://forum.alginkgo.com/go/BuBuq7N0k5

union with his spouse and all like-minded prodigals wherever he found them.

Penitents like him and Malcolm-X admit their errors, then humbly pave the road with bricks of good deeds for the conscious development of sacralized citizens; folks with sufficient grit to establish mature, *Son-of-Man* polities. This is no *'next-year-in-Jerusalem'* fantasy but rather a divinely guided plan of action designed to transform the soul by dying to self-centered ambition on a moment-to-moment basis. If pride or ignorance prevent this repair, we develop deep-seated anxieties with socio-psychopathic leanings towards sadism or masochism. We become *gog* or *magog*-worthy constituents who seek satisfaction in a system that insults its source of grace by celebrating lies and liars. Sadly, our majority joins a camp whose devilry is worse than that of Himmler's *SS* or the Aztec savagery.

real zion

Ideally, the right honorably entrenched habit of daily repentance leads to our soul's resurrection and ascension. Un-jaded, pure-of-heart folks do it innately. ~~Jesus~~ referred to its power of transfiguration by saying; "... *not my will but thine be done.*" As their Messiah, he reminded Jews that the way out of Pharisee (*intellectual*) and Sadducee (*militant*) hell had been lit by the *Decalogue*, not *Talmud*, *Kabbalah* or *Catechism*. Howbeit, his task was not to rule over an unclean Promised Land but rather to guide his disciples to Jacob's Ladder of Ascendance via the *Beatitudes* of Mount Marriage. His disciples are those he will not reject on Judgement Day (Matt.7.21) because they comprise a communion capable of planting and raising good seed by imitating *christos* initiation, for which blood sacrifice has nothing whatsoever to do with except as a major diversion to test our discernment.

Death to selfishness requires no convent, sacrifice, blood-stained whip, or secret seedy sacristy. It is distinctly followed by the phoenix of faith that literally becomes '*the substance of things hoped for as evidence of the unseen*'. This literal component of G-d's covenant with Abraham was reserved for the archetypal example set by Ahmad, and as attested to by the Arian church of Khadijah. They likely knew the *Gospel of Barnabas* and fully expected Ahmad's arrival to complete Allah's promise to Abraham, both figuratively and literally. All else is the hot air of Zionism,[6] Christian and not. Thus did Mohammad established *The Kingdom* that was quickly abandoned within forty-years due to the religio-neuro-politics of Babylon's cultural subversion.

ON ZION

🗝 The fruit born of this branch bears seeds filled with Revelation Knowledge, which is the same Divine Law or Guidance referred to as the "root" of Jesse's *tree of life*, the very same that bore the branch known popularly as ~~Jesus~~, the son of Miriam. This guidance is the law placed in the 'ark'; that is to say, safely deposited in the heart of understanding for those who choose to conform to it. **Zion**—with its symbolic **Tabernacle** (*temple* or *body*) and **Ark of the Covenant** (*heart*)—is the rock of faith activated in an understanding heart. This is to say it is the

---

6. * See ***Forgotten Saints***: The Gospel of Barnabas: Survey and Commentary, 2010, https://forum.alginkgo.com/go/BuBuq7N0k5 // Jerusalem Sion & Zion https://forum.alginkgo.com/go/yPWVkBwKXF

rock or cornerstone of anyone who establishes the *Kingdom of God* by making peace with G-d via contrite submission.

Hence: "*Blessed are the Peacemakers* …" (Matt.5.9). The understanding and activation of this submission, which is optimized in marriage, is Zion. Nothing else needed.

<small>excerpt from *Trinity*, p 109, https://forum.alginkgo.com/go/9z3fNJopca</small>

The case for the Kingdom of G-d thus rests on Chaste Monogamy.

7

PRO-PATRIA
THE PRICE OF ADULTERY

> 🗝 He ate the dog for the sake of an unappeasable patriotic desire in the glow of a great faith that lives still in the pursuit of a great illusion kindled like a false beacon by a great man [Napoleon] to lead astray the effort of a brave nation ... Pro Patria !
>
> Joseph Conrad, *A Personal Record*

the dilemma

Self-centered couplings like the Macbeths, Nero & Messalina, or *Fard & Poole, Ltd.*, lack the buoyant verve and steady hand of resolved purpose commonly seen in the visage of seasoned warriors who stand their ground without imperial design. Like the Vatican, Fard taught his Negroes that allegiance lay elsewhere, and that they were not bound to defend any American homeland. Dualism's dialectic thus favors the *Mystery of Iniquity's* cynic. In this case, and sadly so—precisely as Mr. Conrad stated.

Indeed, for lack of knowledge, *pro-patria* folks self-destruct by assisting the self-centered criminality of elite *DP*-predators. I will show that this is built into spiritual law as a default protocol. The condition's social, moral, and intellectual arrests often lead entire nations into hellishness. To the contrary, after reaching the active rest of King and Queen fishers in communal ponds, well-married folks qualify for the enhanced *christos* development of their respectively gendered Kingdoms in quiet unicity; and this to the exclusion of all who fail to submit or qualify for the grace of its guidance and protection.

Their combined fractals affect wedded transcendence in unity, so that when taken together they result in a more formidable sum due to the gravity of G-d's additional grace. Hence again, a great divide exists between those who do and those who do not qualify for enhancements deriving from sacred fidelity, for which Mr Poole did not qualify (see Q.21.90-96 for *the great divide*).

When a couple is chastely united, divine immanence manifests divine intent, to which end ecstasy faithfully calls the reverent. If you can imagine what bundles of such unions might achieve, you are able to see *The Kingdom*, which is equivalent to seeing G-d, what the Beatitude actually claims (Matt.5.9). Dysfunctional unions cannot fashion a single grail let alone a viable confederacy. Consequently, to save face they keep up pretenses with apologetics for sin and immodesty. When this occurs, Professor Unwin tells us that within three generations all is lost. Every civilization that permitted immodest dress and behavior fell.

If selfishly or materialistically oriented —e.g., marriages contracted to preserve wealth alone— hellish outcomes cannot be avoided, which makes prognostication fairly easy for the sapient. Another matter of import is this:

> 🔑 *Being asked by the Pharisees when the kingdom of God cometh, he answered and said: The kingdom of God cometh not with observation: neither shall they say, Lo, here! or, There! for lo, the kingdom of God is within you* (Lk 17:20).
> 🔑 A more correct rendering is ***in your midst***.

Hence, folks who transcend are *in the midst* of those who don't. Since the latter are the majority, they present a substantial challenge to divinely-inclined kinfolk [1] who transcend the instinctive level of consciousness by intellect to expressly acknowledge *The Great Mystery's* system of apartheid or *great divide*.

Jews are persuaded to think they are at the top of this middens, when in fact the professional organization of furtive or overt plunder is their real faith; most always using someone else's capital, human and not. To the contrary, only humility and the right mate activate sufficient supernal grace to qualify as primal sapience. The true sage allows the circulation of fractal energies to affect beneficial outcomes from unseen realms for all; this is to say, they channel the grace irradiated plasma described by Tesla and Claudio Messori et. al.[2] You know, the unseen stuff that carries *logos*. All such alignments should carry Blue Lodge initiations to our fifth decade.

The supernal grace availed by chaste monogamy

---

1. See: ***The Lost Gospel*** by B L Mack, https://forum.alginkgo.com/go/MhnOr5O65v
2. From Continuity to Contiguity: On the genesis of consciousness, culture and oral language (Part I) https://forum.alginkgo.com/go/DKFxJJfHqZ

requires sufficient knowledge and skill levels to apply what is beneficial while avoiding what is not. Such discernment transcends and transfigures as a complementary process of evolution. On the other hand, non-transcendent unions obtain collective harm(s), so that nations of poorly-matched congregants (*gogs & magogs*) readily submit to randomized bundling by narcissist religionists per Luciferian cults or Ahrimanic tech protocols for the walking dead cyborgs. This is the *pro patria* conditioning that leads to dog eating.

To the contrary, fidelity-acquired transcendence attracts, focuses-on, and actuates top-shelf *EMF*-flux patterns that safely place beneficial fractal bearers in the midst of lies and liars who corrupt all partnerships. I will demonstrate how this is done following a mimetic elaboration on the tomfoolery of *DP*-charlatans like Mr Poole.

forensic oscillations

NOI leaders fit the *Dark Personality* (*DP*) profile of predatory personalities.

1. 🔎 they achieve goals through sophisticated and complex manipulations of people using fact and fiction;
2. 🔎 they prevent the exposure of their deceit by pitting people against each other;
3. 🔎 they expertly masquerade authentic motivation (consummate actors);
4. 🔎 they maintain secrecy of motive.

Perps like Mr Poole zealously guard against any exposure of their selfish pursuits, which puts them in a category far beneath gentlemen like Mr Bumpy Johnson. Hypocrites prevent, damage, or inhibit the flow of supernal grace at all institutional levels. Consequently, redemptive powers governing the community's full potential (*christos*) fail to incarnate. *DP* perps nonchalantly short circuit optimal evolutionary processing in G-d's name:

> 🔑 Such people radiate non-complementary TVC ethers along with radical sub-elemental hadrons that cannot systems-couple to form the required elasticity. They lack the facilitative capacitance to produce, process, apply, and distribute requisite amalgams that obtain satisfaction. Ostentation, celebrity, medallions, and blue ribbon oscars are poor substitutes for supernal grace.
>
> ~ Excerpt: *Sexology For The Wise*

Lobaczewski points out repeatedly that pathocracies always adopt a macrosocial, politically-correct mask of sane normality. Ideology sculpts its facade with a view to conceal the truth while avoiding any "diagnosis" of the system as pathological—that is, as a persistently predatory sociopolitical structure such as Christian or Muslim Colonialism for which chauvinist futility spends *pro patria* dog eaters until death cancels the burlesque. This is a major reason why soldiers caught in its moral conundrum commit suicide. Corrupt leaders shed the metaphysical toxins of propaganda to alter or prevent the reception and/or utilization of beneficial dynamics at sub-atomic watersheds where things unseen become seen. We now know this includes intention. All is tainted.

REFERENCES: 3

EXCERPT, Pokorný, et al.

🔑 Excited longitudinal polar oscillations in microtubules in eukaryotic cells generate the endogenous electromagnetic field. The metabolic activity of mitochondria connected with water ordering forms conditions for excitation. The electrodynamic field plays an important role in the establishment of coherence, directional transport, organization of morphological structures, interactions, information transfer, and brain activity ... The existence of the endogenous biological electromagnetic field, its generation by microtubules and supporting effects produced by mitochondria have a reasonable experimental foundation. Cancer transformation is a pathological reduction of the coherent energy state far from thermodynamic equilibrium. Malignancy or local invasion and metastasis, is a direct consequence of mitochondrial dysfunction, disturbed microtubule polar oscillations and the generated electromagnetic field.

---

3. For an excellent précis of how NOI founders fit DP (*Dark Personality*) criteria, see: Psychopaths: Masks of Sanity, by Harrison Koehli, Political Ponerology (01Oct24).

See: ***Sexology For The Wise:*** Noetic Science https://forum.alginkgo.com/go/NTzOMIeg2i

Messori, Claudio. (2016). From Continuity to Contiguity: On the genesis of consciousness, culture and oral language (Part I of IV). Journal of Consciousness Exploration and Research. 7. 163-177. https://forum.alginkgo.com/go/tQCjryjfcX

Shwabl, Herbert, Klima, Herbert (2005/05/01) Spontaneous Ultra-weak Photon Emission from Biological Systems and the Endogenous Light Field 10.1159/000083960

Jiří Pokorný, Jan Pokorný, Jitka Kobilková, Postulates on electromagnetic activity in biological systems and cancer, Integrative Biology, Volume 5, Issue 12, December 2013, pp 1439–1446, https://doi.org/10.1039/c3ib40166a

Contrition

NOETIC HYPOTHESIS:

🔑 Pernicious spouses, teachers, perverts, and doctrines likely impose *EMF*'s with incompatible Tenso-Vibrational Configurations (*TVC*s) (oscillations) leading to cancer, which is the loss of form, function, and purpose, which is what Al'Qur'an said happened to Adam as a race (Q.20.115).

Violating moral borders is like passing laws against physics and common sense. Incompatible coupling with toxins not only fosters cancer but also invents apologetic traditions for corrupt social institutions. Both fill reservoirs to the brim with altered fractal patterns that manifest harm.

vested blindness

Human sacrifice is a prime example of religious mania that slipped into belief systems as required worship. I'm thinking this occured after Cain revised the worship of Shakti for purposes of organized plunder; to include cannibalistic sublimation rites (communion) with subsequent genocidal proclivities; in G-d's name of course, and with extraordinary leave to commit abject depravity. Similar errors slipped into Islam and Crusaderdom. Indeed, much of the world admits respective and varied prostrations to blind traditions that vest these chairs.

The solution presented herein is a thoroughgoing rinse in waters of contrition followed by resurrection from dead-end visions. Indeed, *"Let the dead bury the dead"* (Lk 9:60). The epiphany so purchased obtains post-rebirth morality and disciplines leading to the ascended transcendence of self-will in concert with divine intent. This is Easter. But it doesn't happen overnight or in three days.

The New Physics of Noetic Science attempts to define unseen subtleties affected by combinations of sub-atomic fractals in complementary communions that facilitate the entire scheme. These dynamics are likely responsible for what we call *blessing* or *cursing* in accord with choices made and words spoken. Since cycloidal rounds of non-complectory futility form the indelible record that many take to the grave, I think it best that we plead for divine redactions before qualifying to enter hell's oubliette.

I posit that heaven's chaste earth policy for monogamous marriage determines far more than sexual congress because it has everything to do with good, evil, and giving lies to the truth that promote the latter.* With this mind, we can now move on to the cosmological implications of what has been existential from the start. Folks who honor leaders like Elijah Poole or Joe Biden on a continuum eventually eat *pro patria* dog food. It is the price of their infidelity.

> 🗝 *The various kinds of adulteries and whoredoms (such as are enumerated in Leviticus 18:6-30), signify various adulterations and falsifications of good and truth ... All adulteries correspond to the adulterations of good and truth.*[4]
>
> ~ E Swedenborg

---

4. https://swedenborg.com
 ALSO SEE: "Until The Eschaton Is Spent" https://www.thinkspot.com/feed/single_post?psid=b5upyz

8

THE SHADOW
WHITE MAN'S BURDEN

🗝 *Verily, they who distort the meaning of Our messages are not hidden from Us (Q 41.40) ...*
🗝 *And tell the men to lower their gaze and be mindful of their chastity. (Q 24.30) ...*

wavelengths

WE HAVE the potential to consciously access and manage greater fields of cosmic energies for our benefit. As receiver-transmitters, we can enjoin ideal cognizance by tuning fractal antennas (DNA) to frequencies that receive and transmit moral turpitude. Prayer helps, but obedience is better. Knowing how to practice this approach to the management of sensory data processing eases our fear of divine abandonment, which sits at the root of all paranoia. Indeed, some blow smoke, some sing and dance; and others light candles, ring bells, and chant. There are many approaches to meditative states that rise above mundane mindlessness.

Moral frequency tuning searches out heaven's wavelength, which is especially difficult in light of modern distractions. We can connect with advancing levels of *logos* reception and refraction, depending on knowledge levels and intent. Whatever method is used, our intention imbues electro-magnetic fields (*EMF*s) with a purpose that extends into cosmos and community, so that imaginations of desired outcomes actually attract responses that help actuate the substantiation of things hoped for (Heb.11:1), whether for good or evil.

Mr. Poole's pretense of morally correct agency reaped destruction because heaven —the abode of judgement— suffers no posturing. Evil or misguided intentions reap whirlwinds in arenas where only the immaculate can and will suffice. Indeed, delusions often allow folks to think they've safely crossed a forbidden chasm to access universal secrets. Meanwhile, helots in Blue Lodges clean streets and change sheets while wiping bottoms and blood in a carnal, war-weary world that fervently pays for zealous mass murdering pretenders on both sides of all divides.

Since this is the story of civilization, and because transcendence is not found in Al'Qur'an, it may be unwise to attend voodoo sublimation rites that promise to please G-d. In street Arabic, 'transcendence' is rendered *gahyr mahdud*, meaning *'without boundaries'*—[thank you Br Hasan-X]. Because the Arabic term is clear and boundaries are sacrosanct, in the interest of divine order over earthly clay and everlasting peace I think it best not to pretend that speculative transcendence is kosher while bottoms need daily wipes. It is wiser to carefully define each adulterous boundary, especially since Al' Qur'an says they are persistently violated by an unrighteous majority in whose midst we dwell.

Contrition

Thinking they crossed the chasm safely, NOI founders went further and conditioned their disciples to proudly carry the *White Man's Burden* as an act of cultural magick. Let us investigate rather than speculate:

🔑 As the movement [NOI] gained vested interests in real estate and commercial enterprises, as well as economic and political weight in Black and White communities, one block of NOI leadership became increasingly conservative and urged the case for maintaining a stable status quo, rather than risk the loss of so much that will have been so arduously gained. They quickly realized that Muslim gains can be protected only while there is a fairly stable White society in America, scornful of mere material and negotiable gains. Clinging to the spirit of the original revelation and holding it capable of continual renewal in each generation, will demand a relentless war on the detested status quo, with its entrenched, White domination. [1]

kismet

🔑 The doubt of sovereign power enthroned in a fixed standard of conduct is the hardest thing to stumble against; it is the thing that breeds yelling panics and good little quiet villainies; it's the true shadow of calamity.

---

1. ~ CE Lincoln, Black Muslims in America (1961, -73, & -94) p 218. https://www.goodreads.com/book/show/1010384.The_Black_Muslims_in_America

SEE: N. TINAZ, "From Periphery to Centre: A Sociological Analysis ... with Specific Reference to Imam W. Mohammed and Minister Louis Farrakhan Communities," Turkish J of Islamic Studies , vol.14, 2006

~ *J Conrad,* Lord Jim

Booty keeping and counting is a conspiratorial 'mystery drama' acted out by Deep State players throughout history. It requires Elysian intoxication and spellbinding smooth talkers. Indeed, its X marked fez-topped bottoms for *Fard & Poole Ltd.*, a partnership that religiously conned thousands of inner-city helots. Suffering from low self-esteem and compounded's ignorance, their legatees, relatives, empathizers, sympathizers and dimwitted offshoots are advised to acknowledge the perfidy in order to access clear waters of prodigal repentance. Otherwise, tempestuous epigenetic vectors and fractals—what Mr. Conrad called *'quiet villainies'*—will, and without fail, foster the hushed *'squandering of selves'* (Q.42.45).

Like registered Democrats and Republicans, NOI gangs played into the hands of everyman's foe, which unavoidably occurs in the absence of divine guidance. Once again, I beg the reader to let evidence and reason speak rather than reactive programming. NOI adepts merely applied ancient protocols (see Appendices: Ibn Maymun) that assured gratification for grand masters of the cult. Business-as-usual myth-mongering merely launched a crusade peopled by unlearned, impoverished Negroes — the great-great grandchildren of marks who were sold by their own chiefs during the best-forgotten days of the never-was Wakanda facsimile of Shaka Zulu's rather large kahunae in honor of Dahomey's celibate Amazons. Nothing normal here, which is precisely where NOI mythoclasty should begin.

However, the existential cause of NOI failure runs in a much deeper vein because chaste conjugal love is the holy grail of authentic spirituality; the latter being morally-inclined, correctly-informed, human consciousness. I suggest that protocols for booty keeping and fez and kahuna counting not only caused a conflagration of X-pseudonyms at NOI's Ten-Dollar-per-new-name exchange counters, but also invited **FBI COINTEL-PRO** blackmail. Pretense in G-d's name collides head on with the Law of Disgrace (Q.5.33). Nemesis is ever ready and forever at the door. Hence, NOI's struggle with the Deep State was not an '*us versus them*' contest but rather 'kismet for hypocrites'. Indeed, NOI's Relationship with the FBI was intimate.

🔎 *If Herbert Mohammed could be removed as successor to the leadership of the NOI, it would place our top level NOI informants in a better position to neutralize the extremist cult.* [2]

This frenetic exercise in dupism happened while Myer Lansky exploited J Edgar Hoover's fetish for cross-dressing. The 33rd degree grand master in chief was then promoted to gay grand inquisitor in charge of America's *Mafia Denial Syndrome*. A simulacrum of special interests led to the recent Epstein Islander Syndrome, noting that Lansky died in Israel's safe haven for international, Mossad-friendly villains.

Our recalcitrance to discuss these matters describes cognitive dissonance. Entire congregations avoid consequent discussions, much like post-WWII Germany. Absent genuine contrition for what really happened, the void fills with apologies for sacralized delusions and doctrines that ease the escape. The national hysteria of this psychosis is

---

2. Gardel, 'Countdown to Armageddon', p 4, Nordic Journal for the Study of Religion; Vol. 31 (1995) ; Temenos; Vol 31 (1995) ; 2342-7256 https://doi.org/10.33356/temenos.6047

typical. It gave honor to a cross-dressing, *DP*-pervert like J Edgar Hoover—the nation's top-cop for forty years—and sealed America's fate by clearing a path for the public assassination of truth.

By microcosmic contrast, NOI's robust mystery drama added hero-worship to its group-think *egregore*, and conned acolytes into adopting an imaginary folk soul. Germany similarly misplaced its trust in the Aryan fantasy that dressed *pro patria* narcissism in garments of Wagnerian romance. Reprobates at such helms demand the ratification of delusions protected by a well-dressed congress of armed thugs. In NOI's case we have Fard's pretended deity and Poole's pretended '*son-of-god*' messiah status. Standing on the platform of this exalted self-worth, they branded congregants with *Bell-Hop*, '*Pullman*' and '*Doorman*' uniforms and dressed their women in conventual habits worthy of St. Theresa. Thus, they kept helot capital in hand. This is what happened. And if you substitute '*Aryan*' for NOI's *Yakub* myth, their microcosm of false hope instantly comes alive with *cultured magick*; which is defined as:

> ... bringing individual members into such a superhuman state of power and awareness that they would be able to exert a magical influence on the world, beginning with fascist state elitists.[3]

the shadow of ur

Like Joseph Smith, Mr. Poole was a soft-spoken fascist

---

3. See: Drury, Nevill (2004). The Dictionary of the Esoteric: 3000 Entries on the Mystical and Occult Traditions. Delhi: Motilal Banarsidass. ISBN 978-81-208-1989-4. (Aug 2022.)

whose cultured magick was nascently managed by speculative Freemasons. He and Brother Malcolm persuaded impoverished inner-city negroes to worship yet another Ismai'ili god-man avatar (Fard). This scheme smacks of several ancient Mystery Religions out of the Middle East; some of which are sourced to the same pens that caused Christians, Jews and Muslims to fall into error on even grander scales.

Fard, whose mother was a Khazar Jewess, took his game plan straight out of Evola's misogynist expose on *Mystery Religion Elitism*. To which he added the immensely successful Catholic scam of Perennialist mysticism, ala *Rene' Guenon* — another Speculative Freemason and goddess idolater. This temple stood in Ur of the Chaldees more than four thousand years ago, and was likely viewed by Abram with contempt. Her followers continued morbid obsecrations long after Sumerian Kings substituted lambs-of-god for infants on her bloody altars, something we have on cuneiform record. Even Evola called his disciples *The People of Ur* in her honor.

Ur's errant fractals became the same lego bricks used to construct the living stones of Sippara's University for the Sepharvaim, whose priests of distraction offered human sacrifice, an Amorite specialty (Gen.15.16). Some of these stones eventually wrote the *Talmud* and the lasting journal of double-speak accounting to check and balance unholy deeds and shekels for the *Sumerian Swindle* ala Central Banking controlled corporations everywhere.

> For the most complete history of fiscal duplicity and usury throughout the ages, see the works of Alexander Del Mar.
> https://forum.alginkgo.com/go/HGXbIZNi1e

Metaphysically, this is no different than China's foray into the cultured magick of semiotics after Christian missionaries broke through the Sino-wall for crypto masters of the craft (think opium & Sassoon). These affiliations descended from more ancient streams of Venetians aligned with the Anglo-Dutch Atlanticist gang that followed the wake of Marco Polo's scam. After further seeding in the west, they became Pepe Escobar's Chabdnik hegemons in league with The City's Deep State 15-minute cities everywhere. Without fail, such dialectical results bring: *i*) the destruction of higher culture; and *ii*) thralldom to mass-murdering thieves who organize civilized plunder for a hushed imperium.

Without the resonance provided by clear waters of contrition, NOI's microcosm remains devoid of authentic ancestral and cultural memoirs that provide a blessedly virile *elan vitae*. Put more succinctly and without restraint, NOI's fertile lies fashioned an evangelical church from dispirited men and women whose living stones were steeped in furtive liaisons and forced abandonment, having been conditioned to do so by four centuries of slavery.

- add intense venereal competition
- mix with endless streams of broken family units steeped in theological accretions of Orientalist and African voodoo;
- promote all the above with false eschatology
- then bake for three generations in an amalgam of dreadful oppression and vain glorious hope

Disingenuous myths and lies easily redirected the aimless drift of justifiable Negro resentments; sentiments that nevertheless stewed in Caucasian-centric modernity.

Contrition

Now imagine these epigenetic *EMF*-fractals after nearly one-hundred years of an accursed aura's interference with circadian, *alpha-wave* oscillations @ 7.87 hz — brimming with occult Shi'ism*. The latter being confirmed by the 'sudden occultation' of Fard, who miraculously began speaking on the phone to Mohammad Ali and other credulous marks, shortly after Fard's arrest for ritual murder in 1934* ... this is pure gypsy Shi'ism on the march.

Although NOI's revision of history supports Al Shariati's Alawite Shi'ism, it likely went undisclosed to Blue Lodged acolytes who called Mr Poole, "*Supreme Leader*", which is the Iranian term. And take note: Master Fard is scheduled to return as Mahdi. This is the shadow of Ur.

- 🔎 Poole believed Farad (Fard) was the Christian Messiah and Islam's Mahdi, but went even further ...
- 🔎 declaring that Farad was 'God in the flesh', and that he, Elijah Poole of Georgia, was the Messenger of God.

references4

---

4. Beynon, E. D. (1938). The Voodoo Cult Among Negro Migrants in Detroit. American Journal of Sociology, 43(6), 894–907. http://www.jstor.org/stable/2768686

E E Curtis (2021) Chapter: "The Nation of Islam". In Handbook of Islamic Sects and Movements. Muhammad A Upal, C M. Cusack (eds) https://forum.alginkgo.com/go/4DBDClPwaR

* Eugene Montsalvat: THE IRANIAN PRECURSORS OF THE FOURTH POLITICAL THEORY, ISSN 2611-626X, Feb 2016 https://forum.alginkgo.com/go/ToOESqwJB3

See also Quisay W (2023). Neo-traditionalism in Islam in the West: Orthodoxy, Spirituality and Politics. p 8. Edinburgh, U Press; https://scholarworks.indianapolis.iu.edu/items/fd24e013-a805-4e41-bc49-22022812873e

9

TRIAL & ERROR
HARUT & MARUT

dividing the spousal auspice

I propose three maxims justified by reason and scripture:

1. Marital Fidelity maintains divine protection and guidance for Kingdom of God polities.
2. Chauvinism is anathema to this purpose.
3. To sustainably manifest *Kingdom Policies*, authorities must not:
   - forbid marriage or make it economically untenable;
   - practice or approve immodesty, promiscuity, infidelity, sexual perversions, or adultery;
   - impose perfidy and/or confusion on the conjoined auspice of heterosexual governance.

Scripture repeatedly indicates that marriage existentially

and definitively challenges our submission to divine will. Moreover, failure to acknowledge and submit to its shared throne confirms the presence of chauvinism's defiant insolence. This includes bigotry stemming from fabricated traditions and corrupt renderings of scripture across a broad spectrum of religious literature. It is this occult aspect, specifically that of Persian Shi'ism, that is under discussion becuase it permeates NOI's worldview. What's more is that much of this stream of superstition derives from the bloody-minded Shaktism of sutee lovers — dating to such dark depths of antiquity that only Akashic masters can comprehend the reach of its demonic vortex. Indeed, we see *as through a glass darkly*, in the words of errant St Paul.

I will now cite two well-known examples of traditional misguidance as typical examples:

- *the coming of Mahdi and the return of Jesus as messianic avatars are not mentioned in Al'Qur'an, yet play a major role in Muslim eschatology.*

- *the Bible's oldest manuscripts make no mention of the trinity; something Erasmus discovered when translating the Vulgate during the 15th Century CE. Almost no one knew. Moreover:*

> Codex Sinaiticus was worked over by correctors long after it was first written, one can actually see this process of alteration for doctrinal reasons at work.

- This 'oldest' copy of the complete Bible also

lacks any of the now published. NT references to Christ's Resurrection.
- 🔎 It bears absolutely no mention of a Resurrected Body' of Christ, or of any of the later additions referring to his many apparitions before his ascension.
- 🔎 Even the ascension itself is absent. [1]

Nonetheless, both schemes are found in the myths of Kali and Shakti fertility cults, out of which derive contemporary Persian makeovers of the ancient mother of god goddess and her infamous Parsee serpent cult. When added to the cultured magick of neuro-politics, pedestrian ascent-to *Rahim* grace is blocked by more than just official lies. Deception is traditional.

Jesus raised this indictment against the rabbins of his day (Matt.23:13). I view the Malcolm-X experience as a parallel refraction that connects America to The Academy of Cultural Misguidance whose first chairs were held by students of *Harut* & *Marut*, who long ago prepared core curricula for the Frankfurt School of Cultural Subversion. Its corporate mission statement or course description could have read as follows:

> SECRETS OF DIVIDING THE SPOUSAL AUSPICE: subversive tactics that leave Semites and Satraps in charge

Harut & Marut, whoever they were, held chairs at Babylon's Sippara University circa 2nd century BCE

---

1. * See: *Secrets of Mount Sinai* https://forum.alginkgo.com/go/pTYoOG MOFF // also *Trinity: The Metamorphosis of Myth* https://forum.alginkgo.com/go/5zVvL07vLe

(Q.2.102). They presented a stellar approach to goy governance after Iskandar reinstated corrupt *pseudo*-Zoroastrian satraps on Persian thrones in regions where exceptional Jewish idolators had been exiled for centuries. Indeed, over time and by the rivers of Babylon where they finally sat down, the preserved syncretic schemes of Old World Amorites were serially transcribed, reformed, and then *Hellenized, Romanized, Catholicized,* and *Urdu-Islamicized* for export, east, west, north and south. Esoterically this culminated in Europe's 19th Century Speculative Freemasonic theosophies ala Gurdjiief, for example, versus Rudolf Steiner's more user-friendly Anthroposophy (esoteric Christianity). Whatever the cult, all were steeped in what became the Kabbalist *egregore* that reclined comfortably in alchemical dens behind castle walls and in Eurasian salons and book stores for centuries.[2]

Thus, religious accretion, doctrinal assumptions such as what Erasmus uncovered, and all parlor attendees remain undiscussed except behind hushed doors. I have held many soirees for Nicodemus-*Church of The Culdee* types over the years. Nonetheless, this aspect of history should not be underestimated or ignored. It is where Victor Hugo's Devilfish everywhere lurks with tentacles at the ready.

Abstract Standard Jewish Encyclopedia [3]

---

2. See: Dunlap, S. F. (1894). The Ghebers of Hebron; https://forum.alginkgo.com/go/dNsbYDs9yp

3. ** Lost Ten Tribes & Babylon Chart: A History of the Jewish People, by H.H. Ben-Sasson,

Also See: Militant Zionism in America: The Rise and Impact of the Jabotinsky Movement in the United States, 1926-1948 https://muse.jhu.edu/article/53701/summary

🔍 In the 1st century BCE a Jewish State was set up around Nehardea by two brothers, ANILAI (Anilaos) and ASINAI (Asinaios), and this lasted for many years. The Jews of Babylon remained in constant touch with the Jews of Israel and even supplied some of their leaders (e.g. Hillel) with arms and supplies. During the Roman occupation, the Babylonian Jews rose against the emperor Trajan, the revolt being bloodily suppressed by his commander, Lucius Quietus in 116 CE.

🔎 Under Persian and Parthian rule, the Jews of Babylon (mostly in Kurdistan) enjoyed an extensive measure of internal autonomy, being headed by an Exilarch who was of Davidic descent and was the king's representative. The community was governed by a council of elders (kahal or Judenrat) ... a community of immigrants and converts who grew up around the academies of the Babylonian Talmud.

The Babylonian Talmud was completed over the next 1000 years or so, making it the religio-neuro-politically seasoned device of choice to facilitate dominant traditions among Jews and Muslims who imbibe Judeo-Christian interpolations. Whenever someone says *Talmud* this is it, especially since it bears the kosher stamp of Maimonides, the pre-eminent Kabbalist and personal physician of Salla'u'din. St Paul was also a Kabbalist, as was Hillel, his mentor. This occult, pan-Zionist pattern of magical thinking extends even to the homeland-mania of Pan-African *Wakanda*, which fantasy separates NOI negroes from the realities of their domestic struggle, much as male chauvinism separates spouses from satisfied fulfillment. Think on it, it will help you mature.

Contrition

enmeshments

Alexander conquered the Babylon of his day but not its lying magi. Like Mr Fard, he needed the Black Fire of their goddess's holy smoke to deify himself in Persian vogue. This high-born malarky actually reset the tone of global governance for all pontiffs of cultured magick, ranging from Rome's Palatine to Henry VIII's divine right to murder his wives. For this reason, genuine Parsee highlanders despise Alexander to this day. Subsequent Imperial platforms have since and serially honored the clay footed idol of Prophet Danial (Dan.2.33). Indeed, vain imaginations take mighty nations as far from *bona fide* spiritual transcendence[4] as intellect can get. Indeed, it is Aztec worthy.

To the contrary, genuine transcendence joins together our conscious knowledge of self and non-self (Koenig), much as a mirror reflects images. Without this awareness of the other, we gaze but comprehend little unless we learn how reflected images are related. If no such effort is made, we grow like a weed without the informed ability to govern or guide our soul's evolution or cosmic integration. Borders fade and chaotic enmeshments flourish.

Like water's ability to absorb the essence of everything it touches, the enmeshment engulfs us. What's more is that when fabrications are presented as truth the soul often doesn't know it has been polluted, resulting in dangerously volatile compounded ignorance. Much as a vaccine pollutes the blood, the lying antigen is dropped behind any line of defense. The mesenchyme may blindly rumble against it, and even disturb the body's peace from thenceforth but without physician or patient having a clue as to what is

---

4. See: Karl Koenig, *The Human Soul*

wrong. They walk about in a fog of proud lies and magnificent ignorance whose roots yield non-reproductive hybrids. Under the forensic management of Dark Personalities, eager acolytes cross forbidden bounds with confidence, only to reap whirlwinds.

NOI's platform planks were hewn from ancient mystery religions, most notably, vulgar fertility rites (Dunlap, op.cit.); timbers that were initially *hinduized*, then *sumerized, babylonialized, egyptized, hellenized, romanized, anglicized*, and, in NOI's case, *Nigger-tized*.

Because Canon Laws govern many lies, they are used to crack the subliminal whips of reactionary compulsion. These beastly statutes are why the entire world speaks the English that *Black's Law Book* cunningly misinterprets. Accordingly, after two millennia-plus of trial and error, couples, races, and religions are goaded into endlessly vying with each other. We contend-with, denigrate, devour, castrate, harm, or become antagonistic opposites rather than apposite complements and partners in charge of promised lands that have been fastidiously cleansed of Humanism's self-idolatry. To the contrary, armed with distempered selfies and political venom, contemporary narcissists are everywhere conditioned to receive and compete for Olympian infidelity medals in several canine divisions.

On the obverse of this festival of lies we find acolytes competing for super-abstinent status. This cadre sublimates sexual desire with pious claptrap, to include pit stops for bishop-to-acolyte spermatophagia;[5] or marriage to angels,

---

5. * See: ***Spermatophagia: The Tantric Eucharist***, Ecclesia Gnostica Catholica: The Eucharist by Clément de Saint-Marcq (1906). Translated by Susanne Williams, Rose A Starr, and Joe Collins, 1998. https://forum.alginkgo.com/go/FyyRAOF7zL

demons, jinn, toys, puppets, robots, and even G-d, which is what St Theresa did during her famous wet dreams. All such nonsense is integral to compound perversions practiced by ancient hysterics *en masse*. These include government approved pedophilia, child sacrifice, showtime bestiality at the 'Games', and the sacralization of temple whoredom that is presently mimed during half-time shows at major coliseums worldwide.

the mystery of iniquity

Destroying the temple of Marriage disrupts and critically impairs civil conjugation in every realm and at every turn:

> 🗝 **Marriage is the pillar of society** *and also of government, business, and the military. Marriage cuts to the very heart of a nation. As goes marriage; so goes the nation ...* **Divorces are steps to the grave** *of a culture and a nation. The study of culture, corporate or private, is the study of marriage.*[6]

Unknown to most folks, including our academic majority, Rome was successfully infiltrated by Babil's rabbinate when Josephus and the Alexanders married into the Flavian clan (think Constantine's family). From that time forward, hoodwinked black-robed brigades have sedulously applied Siparra's Protocols for the Sephardi (*Aboo-Habba* = Arabic for *Sepharvaim*). Eventually, they birthed Colonial Burdens

---

    OTO_Spermo-Gnosis   http://arcane-archive.org/religion/thelema/spermo-gnostics-and-the-oto-1.php
    Also: ***Cain's Creed***, pp 442-5 https://forum.alginkgo.com/go/rSiVukcgS
6. L Wood, Marriage Culture: Seed of Society, Root of Behavior (1994) https://forum.alginkgo.com/go/njubMrAlUz

under Roman Eagles, east and west. Their forked-tongue missionaries soundly and sedulously deliver the systemic pablum of imperial plunder; recently undergirded by Speculative Freemasons.

White trash hoodies across the aisle, however, prefer night raids, Sunday football, pizza, beers, and burning crosses. Meanwhile, Prince Hall wannabees and their many spin-offs—like so many jabbering delegates on a lark—feast on the crumbs of this grand deception. Their vanity finds yet another chest ribbon, ring, medal or pin; another lodge meeting, hat, or convention; another conquest on the corner or in the back alley; another forlorn grave; another wink; another pat on the shoulder; and another dollar for Zion.

Although much about Jews and Jesuits has been written and just as quickly ignored, the most concise and worthy invectives I've read so far come from Louis-Ferdinand Céline, who wrote:

> 🗝 *[they demand] submission to the Jewish ideal, that is to say, of the Jewish race in every domain; cultural, economic, political...*
> 🗝 *the Jew is a dictator at heart ... Democracy is always and above all nothing but a veil for jewish Dictatorship.*

REFERENCES AND HISTORIES 7

Contemporary guardians of this colossal chutzpah mostly

---

7. https://forum.alginkgo.com/go/Q8Xit0WCC4 more are provided in my books: **Hand of Iblis**, **Cain's Creed**, **Sexology**, & **Trust**. https://forum.alginkgo.com/go/yPWVkBwKXF

stem from Jews whose ancestors were never Hebrews. Many followed Jacob Frank's messiah into Counter Reformation glory; especially following Germany's utter humiliation under the idolatry of Hitler's Mystery Religion. Nonetheless, be mindful that crypto-Marranos Jews also established Loyola's manics who've pretty-much managed the globe since WWII's re-ascent of the Knights of Malta; and more blatantly so after the serial assassinations of the Kennedys, MLK Jr, and the right honorable Malcolm-X; each of whom, in their own way, would have stopped the cult's plan to ruin America.

This *Mystery of Iniquity* prevents social cohesion by corrupting *vita-sexualis* at both extremes, yielding either zealous piety or vulgar intemperance, for which chaste marriage and self-discipline suffice to establish G-d's Kingdom. That Jews, Jesuits and Parsee idolators were/are at the helm of this grand civilizational makeover is little understood because no one wants to admit the near universal credulity that has allowed organized evil to orchestrate constant war and devastation. Truth be told, victims are responsible due to a lack of corrective contrition and knowledge (Hosea 4:6). It really is that simple. As for NOI relevance, please be patient. I'm building the case.

Considering Jewish Bankers finance both sides of all wars for the industrial-military complex—now a post-Napoleonic tradition—the following is but a small sample of the perfidy that took the Babylonian Talmud clan 2000 years of sedulous infiltrations, treachery, and re-education programs to accomplish.

- Goebbels was raised and educated in a Jesuit seminary; Himmler, perhaps a Jesuit like his uncle Kurt Himmler (SS Officer & Canon of the Bavarian Court); Fr Stemple, the real author of *Mein Kampf*;

pope-to-be Pious XII served in Germany from 1917 to 1929 (without whom Hitler never would have become dictator); and the famous Knight of Malta, *von Papen.*

- Others were occultists like Karl Haushofer of the Vril; EK Hanussen (aka Herschel Steinschneider), a Jew magus called the 'Count St Germaine of Weimar' (a con man and student of Gurdjieff, who'd been initiated by serpent worshipping Yezids in Kurdistan); Himmler's favorite, Karl Maria Wiligut was the Uiligotis sage of Asa-Uana-Sipp and Ahnenerbe); Himmler's astrologer, Wilhelm Wulff was a Sanskrit expert who justified Aryan star gazing; and Dr. KG Heimsoth, a gay Berliner astrologer, was Ernst Rohm's very personal masseuse.

🗝 This abbreviated list of Jews, Catholics, Jesuits, Gays, Freemasons, Knights of Malta, and theosophical dingbats is impressive and surely contains a substantial component of crypto-Frankist Sabbateans. This is not to mention Himmler's cozy relations with Alan Dulles (Freemason & Knight of Malta), or the occult aspects of Operation Paperclip's MK-ULTRA makeovers. Sabbattean Frankists are a prime example of the most dangerous cult of our times. It is likely they who manage high level, Speculative Freemasonry for even greater Hidden masters of neuro-politricks.

Contrition

19th Century Rothschilds at Prayer

10

MARRIED LANDS
TALES OF THE KABALLAH

smokeless fire

At the helm of the cultured magick that robs our majority of its reason are playboys and scintillating women; folks like Hefner, Drumph & Epstein, and Madonna, Spears & Silverman, et alia. But these are mere officers of the line. They are not deeply seated rear admirals or owners of the fleet. All celebrate late night or half-time cheerleading (Q.34.34) for nations who fire bomb innocents in Dresden, Cambodia, Maui, or Palestine for profit. Gershom Scholem says they are deeply immersed in infidelity, mostly because the Kabbalah instructs them to search for the *divine spark* that G-d either lost or hid in sin during Adam's creation. Apparently G-d made a mistake and needs their help, so they've decided to fix it like Jimmy Saville, the king's friend.

 Its Queen-of-Heaven cult honors Black Madonnas like Isis, Kali and Beyoncé; all associated with Egypt's Black Sun, which is nitty-gritty grist per *Ain Soph* of the Lurianic Kabbalah, ala Chabbadnik Talmudists. It is sometimes represented as a closed or blackened, all-seeing-eye, sometimes called the Black Sun, which is intimately associated with Hitler's SS Occult Bureau. Of these several imaginations, Isis symbolizes the luminiferous ether of smokeless Black Fire, reputed to be a subtle emanation of the divine energy G-d managed to lose while meticulously creating the world(s). Prepossessed by this imagination of messianic purpose, they offer it as the light Speculative Freemasons seek but never find.

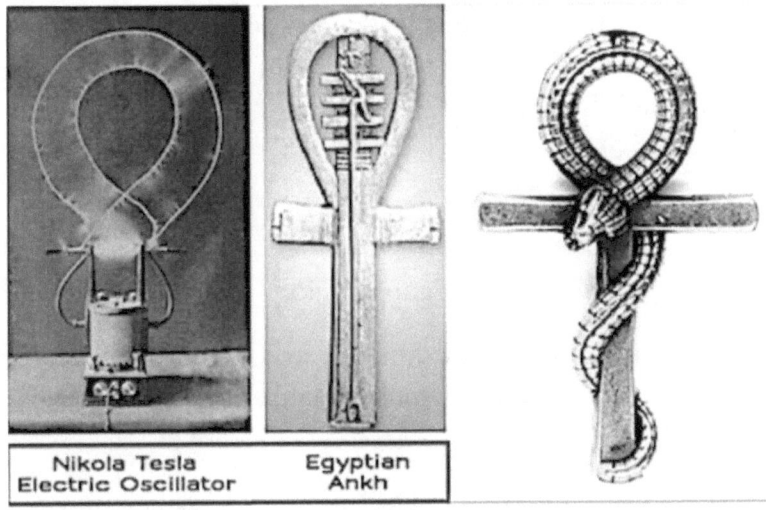

Nikola Tesla Electric Oscillator | Egyptian Ankh

Courtesy of Robert Sephyr

Perhaps associated with the djinn force (*qareen*, Q.15.26) or with Wilhelm Reich's orgasmatron, there is little doubt that Tesla's energy arc represents metaphysical truth. Even so, reckless spirits have great fun playing speculative games with such facts. Reportedly, the highest adepts of this art attend to White Tantra's lost-fire retrieval program with pious orgies. Others self-castrate like the god Attis, Cybele's forlorn lover, she being the madonna of all goddesses, as well as his grandmother after becoming a man, according to some myths. Still others remain celibate to prove themselves worthy of grace by freeing themselves from sexually-charged lost sparks of divinity.

Luciferians prefer to harness Kali's kundalini in order to gain illuminative powers over nature and neighbors. But there's a fine line between this art and that of Gandolf the White. with this in mind I'm thinking it was the dark Ain Soph premise that persuaded the Rhadinite Khagan to convert his band of hearty land pirates to Judaism; mostly because the Talmud grants Jews a *carte blanche* imprimatur to do anything they want to non-Jews. But what has all this to do with NOI? ... patience — wait for it.

1

REFERENCES FOR SERIOUS STUDENTS

dark communion

Intoxication and Elysian fantasies accompanied protocols used by magi like Ibn Maymun, Sinan, and Hasan Al Saba,

---

1. The Khazar Khaganate: https://forum.alginkgo.com/go/iuXn7NTR76

Youvan, Douglas & Virgo, Qaie. (2023). The Khazar-Rothschild Continuum and the Hidden Hand of History. 10.13140/RG.2.2.11838.46401. https://forum.alginkgo.com/go/M7XY13wWhW

Sexology For The Wise: The God Of Plunder, p 414). https://forum.alginkgo.com/go/WT65DjLFk5

Tim Kelly and Russ Winter Discuss Sabbatean Frankism's Impact on the World, https://forum.alginkgo.com/go/lG8v2kTIpE

Neusner, Jacob. The Journal of Modern History, vol. 48, no. 2, 1976, pp. 316–20. JSTOR, http://www.jstor.org/stable/1879832. Accessed 23 Nov. 2024.

also: Gershom Scholem, The Holiness of Sin (1971) https://forum.alginkgo.com/go/M7XY13wWhW

to manage the organized evil of their Assassins and clans. Adam Weishaupt discovered these guidelines and then reapplied them to revitalize his failing *Illuminati* gang, after which they led a successful Counter Reformation that finally ended Rome's struggle with Odin's stubborn oaks in *Germania*. These same neuro-political principles of Deep State subversion spawned the Fatimid Empire and provided pretexts for the Crusades that followed. Indeed, it seems even Schiller knew of Ibn Maymun.

Nonetheless, while I worked among well-qualified scholars and grad students for several years as a lecturer at Islamic universities in Malaysia, I never met anyone who knew this aspect of Islam's history. It is ignored. So deep runs this vein of subversion. The short of it is that the world has inherited the corrupt Parsee fire worship one sees at the Olympics and at altars and national cemeteries everywhere. It is the same faith that caused G-d to erase the Annunaki about 7,500 years ago with Noah's flood.

As for NOI: their re-education initiations follow rites and protocols designed for Speculative Lodges, all of which are corrupt. This includes Prince Hall, Moorish, or any permutations post-1717 AD in particular. Think of it as washing 'old money' and devolving its influence as a sound investment strategy. This is what titled *Black Nobility* did; blue bloods out of Lombardi-Venetian-Latin-Etruscan-Persian and high-born Far East mobs of the Old SilK Road, pre and post-Alaric. They deem lies and liars worthy of honor for purposely misguiding earth's pedestrians for profit, no matter the cost to others. These architects design, operate and legslly own *The Beast* (gog) that sits upon the waters (magog) (Rev.17.1).

This epigenetic *Mystery of Iniquity'* requires the organized betrayal of trust, as tauted by post-Ice Age conmen,

East & West, North & South. It is indelibly anchored to treachery and restively haunts NOI's core with Machiavellian intrigue. Lobaczewski called its bedeviling spirit *"controlled pathological egotism"* in his landmark book, *Political Ponerology*; which is required reading for graduate sojourners. Its haughty dementia—albeit, with greater sophistication—also fits Ignatius Loyola's black-robed gang. Couched in the core of the profound sinistrations that bind such rings to iniquity, you will find infidelity. It is the nidus of impurity.

Conjugal discipline is what evolves and ennobles us as homo-*sapient*-sapiens. But to understand the depth psychology of infidelity, we are forced to admit narcissism because it is what drives practiced sadists like Poole. He impregnated several teenaged girls assigned as personal *"secretaries"* during NOI's early and very busy expansion spawned by brother Malcolm's golden wit. To save face once their bellies grew, Poole had three of them publicly humiliated and banished, along with the children, much in a fashion worthy of Plymouth Rock Puritans. The self-centered cruelty of such a heart runs deep, but the blind credulity of apologist accomplices (*magog*) runs even deeper, which is why compounded ignoramuses seeking to escape divine accountability submit to such cunning cads. Pride runs them straight into that abyss. So beware. They are dangerous.

And remember, if not for G-d's grace (Q.24.21) most of us would remain lost in the same fabricated mysteries that misguided Poole's ancient fertility cult. Indeed, the path of damnation described by Virgil describes folks who are prepossessed by vain imaginations of a life-ideal; who slowly, steadily, certainly, and blindly distribute the circus bread of false hope sold by priests of deception.

Contrition

Idolatry's lavishly appointed arrest of spiritual development thus imbues social milieus with the pomp of Roman power at the podium. Thus, Farrakhan. Pompous denial allows us to cheer barbarous consuls who efficiently mass murder innocents in defense of zionist democracy. Thus, thoroughly conditioned *pro patria* people glibly celebrate the usurpation of dominions and lives belonging to *others*. (🗝) I suggest this represents chutzpah's dark communion. They are sadists (gog) served by mobs of compoundedly ignorant masochists (magog), to include Shi'ites, for example, who typify the masochist sentiment yearly on a bloody march to flog themselves more passionately than Jesuit penitents.

🗝 Christianity includes a long history of masochism – the imprint is of Christ on the cross and the examples are of the thousands of martyrs where there is the voluntary acceptance of violence being imposed upon oneself for the greater glory. The masochistic desire of being the slave or the sacrifice stems from the very act of 'humility' that every Christian is encouraged to practice. Humility becomes a means to deeply unite, wherein the subjection of oneself is to a greater power.

REFERENCES

the law of rahim grace

Scripture encourages us to legitimately inhabit and endorse human supremacy and unity on earth as *"married lands"* (Isa.62.42). This infers clay bodies that are figuratively and intimately united with *logos* with a partner sharing *one flesh* unicity. Numerous passages suggests the following carefully paraphrased passage:

> 🗝 We fittingly incarnate you as conjoined governors over creation, male and female. We compel you to marry so you will choose true guidance by way of conscious experience, and thereafter communicate with Us via the intimate covenant of transcendent coitus.

This is why Al'Qur'an says the following:

> 🗝 Tell the believing men to lower their gaze and guard their private parts. That is purer for them. (Q.30:31)

Because marriage is sacred we should think on it and remake our beds by dressing modestly. So stop fussing over rituals and immodest customs that serve the purposes of *gog & magog*. Al' Qur'an makes it clear that this is what is wrong with the world, as demonstrated by the following erudite revision:

---

2. See: Biale, D. (1982). Masochism and Philosemitism: The Strange Case of Leopold von Sacher-Masoch. Journal of Contemporary History, 17(2), 305–323. https://forum.alginkgo.com/go/gBKP2JEeJ4 // Omar Zaid, Trust: It's Misplacement & Ontogeny https://forum.alginkgo.com/go/8WkEa0Cp8Y

"It becomes a state of prohibition (حرام) imposed upon those communities (على قرية) whom violation of our laws have sunk into disgrace and oblivion (اهلكناها), that they can't regain their former status (يرجعون), unless the perpetrators of corruption in their societies (ياجوج و ماجوج) are conquered/overcome (فُتحت) and they are plucked apart from all higher posts of power and authority (من كل حدب) and thrown away by cutting into pieces (ينسلون)." 🔑 Q.21:95-96

"قالوا يا ذا القرنينِ ان ياجوجَ و ماجوجَ مفسدونَ فى الارضِ"
"They said : "O Zal Qarnain, indeed *Gog* and *Magog* are the perpetrators of chaos and unrest in our land." 🔑 Q.18:94

https://forum.alginkgo.com/go/ji2xroQtGb

Al'Qur'an teaches that *gog* & *magog* are idioms that represent a powerful elite gang whose interest is to keep the land full of chaos and violence. Every nation has criminals who cling like desperate sucklings to seats of power. They need to be plucked away from all provision and thrown on the middens … in pieces. Only then can society look forward to bringing peace and prosperity to its people.

> 🔑 Gog = Deep State elite untouchables called Olympians by intel services

> 🔑 Magog = enablers: their gendarmes, bureaucrats, obeisant taxpayers

anathema

From all perspectives, including science and depth psychology, scripture indicates that the *Law of Rahim Grace* requires faithful refraction of its complementary energies (light). G-d commands us to consciously redirect *logos* with a view to manifest good fruit per covenant relationship with *Him* via marriage. Passively appointed to the task, for epigenetic reasons this makes us assistant creators who consciously walk the transcendent path. That's the plan. It is the meat and drink of authentic communion and has nothing whatsoever to do with crosses, crescent moons, or pot bellied priests, monks and mullahs with prayer beads. Ergo, be it austere celibacy or prudish puritanism, both counter divine intent with devil's play.

Prurient religious extremes find hushed harems filled with sacred courtesans dressed in the robes of ancient fertility rites. This refraction of *"insignificant light"* is what moon worshippers do, and is clearly cited by Moses in the book of *Genesis*. This is the light that Elijah Poole focused on his secretaries after his *nafs al-lawwama* felt secure enough to get away with it, which occurred after Malcolm-X inspired NOI's economic advance.

It is the *"Significant Light"* of this grace that prompted Brother Malcolm's protean spirit. But what is it? Returning to the source, my personal study of the Book of Genesis caused me to conclude that events discussed therein are a re-creation that followed some unimaginably ancient catastrophe:

🗝 The stellar bodies referred to are allegorical and have nothing to do with our solar system.

🗝 The original Hebrew translated as *sun* and *moon* literally invoke 'significant' and 'insignificant' luminaries, respectively.

🗝 G-d placed them in the heavens on the fourth day, the day after grass, herb and fruit trees were created.

🗝 The word *heavens* means '*the Abode of Judgment*' ... the same definition offered by Lao Tse and Confucius.

Linear thinking doesn't work here, but pious masochists the world over are ever ready to whip themselves and others into frenzied mobs at a moment's notice whenever confronted by reasoning that countermands foolishness. After much consideration, I propose that Gen.1.1-3 is more accurately rendered as follows:

🗝 *From the best (first fruits), Elohim shape the abode of judgment and the firm place.*

🗝 *The firm place came to pass waste and empty; and darkness was upon the countenance of deep places as the breath of Elohim brooded over the waters.*

🗝 *Elohim said: 'Become Light', after which fire (judgment) came to pass.*

🗝 *Elohim inspected the light (judgment), that it was good, and set the light apart in the midst of the darkness.*

My position is that marriage is the sanctified vessel for this light and that Elijah Poole's multiple violations of this sanctity is anathema to honor.[3]

---

3. SEE: ***The Hand Of Iblis***, pp 289-290 https://forum.alginkgo.com/

go/BdW6eMMbco

11

TSING
HETEROSEXUAL LOVE MESSAGING

bose-einsteinian operations

ANCIENT CHINESE SAGES called the supra-sophisticated biodynamic systems of reproductive sexuality *Tsing* (*kundalini*). The Qur'an calls its source, *kun-fia-kun*; loose translations of the Bible call it *logos;* and lost Kabbalist Jews call it *Ain Soph.** Whatever it is, we are its living results, each one 'a word made flesh'. The latter dynamics autonomously compel us to survive by way of *Tsing's* sub-atomic '*systems coupling*'. This processing occurs at the *plasma-level* where light interfaces to materialize existential stuff, and this via complementary *EMF*s that affect all biological elements. With nothing less than miraculous attention to innumerable details, these photons, in ways yet known, activate life-giving, sustaining, and renewing bio-chemical exchanges.

These life-driving, Bose-Einsteinian operations sustain our earth-bound identity until death. In the meantime, their radiant dynamics shed earth-bound fractals and formative forces that mysteriously direct our DNA to construct, maintain, and renew our soul's clay-bound house. Indeed, it is a Great Mystery.

At the cited sub-atomic watershed, condensates allow independent bio-dynamic systems to share complementary energies even across a vacuum. And because atoms are immaterial, we are permitted to imagine *Ein Soph's* emanations (per *Kabballah),* possibly as the resonant sound waves that precede the manifestation of light as mentioned in the Vedas and Genesis. The fact that resonance has formative effects in the material universe is now without doubt. And remember, we do not hear all frequencies.

The New Physics of Claudio Messori, *et alia* [1] reveals unseen paths that allow what appear to be intelligent *inter-* and *trans-*dimensional data flows that variably manifest as material and/or psychic intention; vectors that some practitioners of magick call *egregore,* and what others call the neuro-political mindset of groupthink. All such dynamics have a hand in the development of seven discrete life-drives[2] that prod us not only to survive but also to validate our identity. Altogether this describes a compulsion to reiteratively broadcast complementary male-to-female communications *(solat).* This love messaging includes intellectual *(agapeo),* emotional *(fileo),* and conjugal *(eros)* signals.

> * Logos: Greek metaphor for Cosmic-Christos or sun-god messiah; first used in Hebrew literature by Philo of Alexandria (1st Cent BCE)

Ideal heterosexual pairing requires complementary

---

1. https://independent.academia.edu/ClaudioMessori
2. ** See: Hasith Ashan, (2024) The Seven Drivers of Existence, https://forum.alginkgo.com/go/7AZNOQfOvt

tensor-vibrational configurations (*TVC*s) that accommodate the completion of 'systems-couplings' for all three realms of human love (*agapeo, eros, fileo*). What's more is that chaste monogamy provides a unique opportunity for unitarian access to additional grace across a void that autonomously fills with favorably disposed '*things unseen*'. Freedom-setting truth (John.8.31-32) aids these seven drivers by providing celestial insight (guidance). No prayer carpets, candles, or birthday-reveal parties needed. Complementary *TVC*-dynamics provide positive, health-maintaining *EMF*s when congruent, so that our favorably disposed sacralized temples become naturally inclined to maintain the grail of fidelity. Sadly, the inverse also holds, so that non-complementary, unfavorable dynamics incongruently bring negative, unholy outcomes.

configurations

Nature prefers a continuum of congruent **T** *enso* **V** *ibrational* **C** *configurations* (*TVC*s) to accomplish sub-atomic systems-coupling to yield superior outcomes arising from optimized sub-atomic, plasma-level biodynamic photon-exchanges that guide robust bio-chemical transactions towards healthy development and reproduction. What's more, our conscious realization of destiny is preferred to walking-dead surrender to fatalism—which is the jaded alternative our majority accepts when justice and contrition go wanting. This is not "*life more abundantly*" as spoken of in John.10:10; but it does reverberate with post-apocalyptic, zombie-filled landscapes.

Moreover, because practice perfects discipline, the longer one walks the path of fidelity the better human one becomes. This goal is peculiar to the sage, whose clearly regulated gendered system of *logos*-coupling obliges them to periodically throw off the mundane in a fit of happy passion. All things soberly considered, including the undignified acts of love to which we happily submit, chastity suits those who reverently embrace the conjugal bed. A marriage formed in this mold manifests superlative systems-couplings for all three love levels, (*agape, eros, fileo*).[3] Fortunate spouses regularly collapse in a helpless heap of bliss while coming to know each other biblically across a void that separates sovereign souls. Now that's intergalactic travel.

Coital joining expresses unrepressed instincts on consummation, which, in turn, opens portals to receive supplemental grace. The soul awakens to enhanced cognition and becomes nourished by an otherworldly elixir that reciprocally nutrifies and purposefully maintains the *other* for the sake of unicity. Their 'Kingdoms Within' form a confederacy of equal partners who recognize and honor the need to do this for each other's sake. Thus, unity in peaceful complementarity with our most trusted companion is a literal confederacy of "one-flesh peacemakers"(See: Gen.2.24; Matt.5.9 & 19.5). It is this sacred trust that immaculately incarnates *logos* as authentic monotheism.

Blessed afterglows permit each partner to embrace ecstasy with a stamp of divine immanence, which is why we instinctively refer to love as 'heavenly' because that's what it is when love is righteous. Settle for nothing less. Its protective aura considers each respiratory cycle a precious allotment of grace. For this reason and more, and long before vulgar corruptions, Hindis called the vagina **'*yoni*'**, meaning a ***sacred place*** where the making of chaste *TVC-*

---

3. See: Omar Zaid (2024). ***Your Closest Neighbor*** https://forum.alginkgo.com/go/dU5d6AS647

heart-to-heart EMF-imbued memories manifest faith because Allah designed sexual intimacy as the **chalice** that secures, confirms, and matures not only products of conception, but also us. Thus, trust is indelibly cast in the mold of conjugal chastity with absolute fidelity.* All else is flawed.

There is is but one spouse who completes this journey with us should we be afforded the good fortune; just as there is but One God who designed its heart-to-heart, DNA guided, corpuscle-to-episome, life-processing protocols for the management of fractals by the gazillions. Should we one day think that someone '*is the one*', the imagination ignites a flux of unseen dynamic sparks; of pre-matter substrates we can't even begin to describe yet subliminally and compulsively seek to apply.

lgbt, permittivity, polygamy

Venereal passion stamps each faithful union a microchurch. Its confederacy is best actualized when consciously submitted to the 'permittivity' of G-d's plan for moral civility. Permittivity has everything to do with capacitance, which has everything to do with the use of energy, all of which is divinely sourced. The problem Noetic Science confronts is that of sin, which contaminates and restricts what physicists call variable permittivity and ballistic energy flows within *TVC-EMF*-plasma realms. Researchers vigorously search for a fundamental commonality even as I suggest that chauvinism, be it gender, religious, or political, prevents such an advance. Moreover, I think our resistance to permittivity can be measured with greater reliability than a lie detector.

Although the Bible calls chaste monotheist devotees daughters *of-Zion* or *of-Jerusalem*, etc., we must remember that metaphorical and allegorical terms have very little to do with the Talmudic Judaism that forever threatens peace. The latter's chauvinist ranting is indeed exceptional and can be traced to the organized political evil of rabbins who studied under *Harut* & *Marut*; which, if I am correct, was the very first Deep State Academy for *Gog's* high-minded round tables and Tavistockian think tanks.

The chaste commonality herein called for comprises conjoined complements of monogamous fidelity that transmit truth fractals; reiterations of which pour torrents of clarity into each better-informed generation to maintain the holy grail of peaceful communion. Even if unaware of this purpose, a morally fit but naive' couple's intoxicating radiance will autonomously craft home and hearth to bless others, even at the lowest social echelon. However, I suspect the inverse induction of hell's deluded path occurs when systems-couplings are morally unfit or otherwise corrupt. If left uncorrected, they become black holes.

It appears to this writer that the archetypal model of transubstantiated transformation really is this simple. Hence, taking this entire process as a per-gospel metaphysical scheme, we deduce that the informed purity of reverent marriage constitutes the *agapeo* of human being, that of living *in-the-world* while realizing it (matter) is not our source. This indicates that intention affects the manifestation of *logos* because *logos* is what divine intent is. Hence, knowing this increases our capacitance or permittivity (desire/will) to do good; noting however, that the inverse is also true; meaning that if we believe matter is our source, nihilism follows. Consequently, beneficial systems-coupling with G-d-consciousness produces amalgams that continually reap beneficial outcomes, which, over time, and as professor Unwin discovered, enhance goodnesses that reliably derive from complementary gender attributions that support high cultural mores — those that mature sapient ascendence. Cultural subversion opposes this ascendence in favor of materialism or self-centered, Luciferian intent.

Hence, polyamory is less-than-ideal because it compounds confusion. Even worse outcomes are expected when lewd concupiscence, lechery, and sexual perversion attend communal decision makers. Vice removes dignity and forbids sustainable social efficacy from the table of conjugal meat and drink—especially for dissolutes or gays and lesbians who cannot accomplish male-to-female, face-to-face 'systems-coupling' in sub-atomic watersheds of vital plasma-induction zones. Albeit, they can and do mime gender attributions because they have no choice in the matter, as there are only two. However, as non-complementary *TVC*-holders, they can never actually be what they mime.

LGBT *EMF*s do not satiate. Neither do they compare with the unicity of chaste, heterosexual monogamy. Moreover, because *EMF*-flux-phantoms are forever unrequited in the absence of compatible *TVC*s, they remain promiscuous and invariably search for an impossible match. Misgendered brains offer an incongruous biochemistry (see *Sexology*, op.cit.) that disallows the complementary *systems-couplings* that inherently grant access-to and govern the many layered after-glows of authentically requited bliss. Sadly, they cannot qualify for entry into the Kingdom as bride or groom unless humbly and chastely assisting qualified heterosexuals with full knowledge of their limits. They must never be allowed to take the helm of governance over heterosexuals. In this regard, President Trunp is righteous.

Hollywood painfully constructs facades for couplings that are monovalent even though they cannot *zen-fully* meet apposite quantum requirements. It's simply impossible for LGBT ethers (plasma) to direct the formation of complementary amalgams that compatibly or effectively pair in temples (bodies) that have been adversely constructed or modified. Distressed temples such as a genetic male with a feminized brain or vice versa (see *Sexology*)—result from impositions during embryonic development, be they toxic and/or criminal.[4] Thus, with few exceptions, less than thirty-percent (<30%) of LGBT folks are amenable to healing via contrition and rigorous psychotherapy. The near-70% balance are born with incongruent gender-orientations and can never become one flesh with a partner, nor can they meet *face-to-face* during mutual orgasms, which distinctly signifies the handicap.

Although naturally congruent, the same dysfunction stands for illicit heterosexual affairs and/or couples with emotional incompatibilities or aberrant personalities, or polygamous attempts to form an impossible whole. Epigenetically, all impact *eros*, *fileo* and *agape* in a less than optimal ways, with some being more pathological than others. And this is not to mention forced marriages whose public visage is less than inspiring. Such folks should never be permitted to rule over a well-adjusted, heterosexual majority.

We must take care to never devalue, repress, pollute, or upstage a decision-making chair that requires a well-matched pair of circumspect heterosexual spouses who possess, join, and enjoin pure intention with informed wisdom. Poseurs like Fard & Poole or Obama simply wont do, although the cultural magick they employ is like a teddy bear that comforts the darkness of their insignificant focus,

---

4. See ***Sexology For The Wise*** : Vol II. Metaphysics https://forum.alginkgo.com/go/WT65DjLFk5 for causes of LGBT incongruence.

especially for Blue Lodge underclasses the world over, upon whom they prey.

So tolls the bell of *tsing*.

AL QUR'AN ON PAIRS

)وَمِن كُلِّ شَيْءٍ خَلَقْنَا زَوْجَيْنِ لَعَلَّكُمْ تَذَكَّرُونَ (٤٩): 51:49

🗝 And in "EVERYTHING" have We created "PAIRS", so that you may keep it in mind in your deliberations.

وَأَنَّهُ خَلَقَ الزَّوْجَيْنِ الذَّكَرَ وَالْأُنثَىٰ :53:45

🗝 And HE is the One who has created "PAIRS" consisting of the masculine and the feminine.

فَاطِرُ السَّمَاوَاتِ وَالْأَرْضِ ۚ جَعَلَ لَكُم مِّنْ أَنفُسِكُمْ أَزْوَاجًا وَمِنَ الْأَنْعَامِ أَزْوَاجًا: 42:11

🗝 Creator of the Earth and the heavans, WHO has made for your benefit PAIRS out of your selfs, and PAIRS among animals.

وَالَّذِي خَلَقَ الْأَزْوَاجَ كُلَّهَا وَجَعَلَ لَكُم مِّنَ الْفُلْكِ وَالْأَنْعَامِ مَا تَرْكَبُونَ: 43:12

🗝 And HE is the one WHO created PAIRS of "everything".....

سُبْحَانَ الَّذِي خَلَقَ الْأَزْوَاجَ كُلَّهَا مِمَّا تُنبِتُ الْأَرْضُ وَمِنْ أَنفُسِهِمْ وَمِمَّا لَا يَعْلَمُونَ (٣٦) 36:36:

🗝 Glorious is HE Who has created PAIRS of all that the Earth grows, and from their own beings, and "from those things" too of which they do not know about.

SEE: Aurangzaib Yousufzai, *The Divine Wisdom Behind The Creation of "Everything" in "Pairs"*

12

DARK MATTERS
THE METAPHYSICS OF SEX

magic versus *magick*

IN SUM, a properly consummated, preserved, and matured heterosexual marriage continually accesses *rahim* grace at sub-atomic interfaces where unseen precipitations of *logos*-charged plasma materialize virile *TVC*-guided fractals for quantum-level *systems-coupling* with increasing capacitance for the permittivity that enhances phase-transitions that contribute to healthy and prosperous evolutionary processes … whew!

Over time and stage-by-stage, these events accumulate reservoirs of clear water provisions for our good, here and hereafter. In turn, these energies are consciously employed for the robust growth, healing and development of humanity's transformative evolution. This is the grist of what materializes sapience, versus obsessive purification rites that cover lax approaches to justice.

Transformative determinants comprise quantum substrates that derive from energy, dark and not. We know they exist but do not yet fully comprehend their nature. When enabled and properly channeled as described, they `combine to form, recreate, rejuvenate, and maintain life out of *things unseen*, of which we are extensions, perhaps involuted evaginations.* They derive from a place where rivers of clear-waters irradiate everything with *kun-fia-kun logos*, as mentioned in both Genesis and Al Qur'an. Thus, there is no supernatural realm, only a divinely appointed unseen aspect of creation that encompasses everything.

This unseen realm amounts to >95% of what we do not as yet know about our universe. So then, we admit the following:

> 🗝 fractal substrates and forces proceed from only *G-d-knows-where* into our reproductive core with a view to identify, approve, establish, and evolve connections (*solat*/communion) between body, soul, mind, and all of creation.

With this overview in mind, we can now attend the science:

> 🔍 The 'double dark' cosmological model (dark energy & matter) indicates that 30-40% of all matter cannot be seen (no light reflection), and estimates that dark matter outweighs visible matter by at least 10:1. Furthermore, there is evidence that so-called universal constants are not absolutely constant, and that certain chemical processes are directly affected by astrological constellations. Moreover, less than 2% of the universe is visible.
>
> 🔍🔍 Since we have yet to explain 95% of what remains undetermined in the universe—i.e., of what we know is incomprehensible but coherent forms of invisible matter, including *negative inertial mass*—scientists now give serious attention to 'dark matter' in terms of parallel

universes inhabited by 'dark matter' cryptids that interpenetrate and and even manifest in the measly 1% of the universe we do comprehend.

🔍🔍🔍 We have barely scratched the surface of creation's mysteries and best watch our step, because we "don't know our universe at all. [1]

We therefore also admit the following

🗝 that venereally bio-resonant *systems-coupling* of what is clearly gendered DNA exists;

🗝 that plasma energies cross-over resonant *EMF*-curtains and voids between sexual partners to affect, direct, precede, and follow every biochemical exchange and outcome, for better or worse;

🗝 that outcomes with different and particular results depend on circumstances, partners, determinants, and events; to include, for example, rape *versus* rapturous love, or curative herbs versus allopathic toxins.

THEREFORE

▶ A conjugal couple forms a uniquely singular unicity.

▶▶ Under impure conditions, and short of exceptional circumstances,* Bose-Einstein *Prima-Materia* will not admit the Significant flux of supernal, rahim grace.

---

1. Dr Simeon Hein 2024 https://www.youtube.com/watch?v=xfitPZca2G0

Contrition

▶▶▶ Such a deficit is sensed (hungry ghost).

▶▶▶▶ Hence, and especially considering human intention, the additional favor of *Rahim Grace* does not enter or invigorate *EMF*-flux streams containing traditionally-corrupt, epigenetically-transferred, *EMF*-dynamics.

▶▶▶▶▶ Lies and less than honorable intentions and outcomes forbid the supra-natural alchemical processing of beneficial plasma in unholy ground (clay).

Stay with me. Here we are talking magic versus *magick* because if by your tongue or pen you prevent blessing you curse by default. The figurative language of subtle scriptures makes this comprehensible in scientific terms.

> 🗝 <u>For Example:</u> this is why Moses was commanded to remove his sandals because they carried the dust of reprobate traditions that ~~Jesus~~ told his disciples to shake off their feet (Matt 10:14). He did not want corrupt epigenetic vectors to enter his flock.

When properly understood this means the only grace left for liars and their followers is what is common to all, and even this becomes negatively affected by the accumulation of evil intent and outcomes that are incongruent with nature. The worst such results occur under chauvinist and/or criminal auspice, especially when bio-dynamic phase transitions suffer couplings with incompatible mates and/or circumstances; which then gives room for greater evil and loss of proper function. This is the essence of cancer.

> * 🔑 NB: A South African prostitute testified that she and her colleagues specifically prayed to Allah to be spared the HIV virus because their men forced them into prostitution. Since they did this to feed their children. All contracted the virus, but none became ill, this became a curiosity for medical experts who remain flabbergasted. This indicates that The effective prayer of a righteous man or woman availeth much. (James, 5.16)

Although NOI founders did much good for their immediate communities, they also planted epigenetic seeds of grim calamity. Any descent into cultured magick negatively affects *logos* plasma coherency across the board. From neutrinos and muons to pulpit and presidential palace, this has everything to do with what some call ritual purity; hence, some Jews have it correct. However, should goys likewise become obsessively compelled, Jews would surely lose their exceptional status because without non-Jews to prey on, they would founder like all parasites. Therein is the differential.

honorable epigenetics

Allah does not create trees that produce good and bad fruit; nor does He sanction prophets who murder students who expose perfidy. Mr. Poole's infidelities and metaphysical misdirection thus became a heritable epigenetic flux of corrupt fractals that, to this day, continues to saturate legatees with fantasies that flow downstream like holocaust lies. Had he remained faithful to the Right Honorable

Mrs Poole, there surely would have been a different outcome.

> 🔑 The genome can take centuries to change, but with epigenetics, the physiological response cannot only be immediate but also present with lasting effects. We certainly know that human experiences affect how our genes are expressed.
>
> ~ Moshe Szyf, geneticist & molecular biologist, McGill Univ.

Following contrition, the rahim grace under discussion became available to the right honorable Malcolm-X; albeit, minus worldly peace due to the binding covenant he personally made with Poole, his unrepentant mentor. Their relationship was conditional. Polygamy presents a similar conundrum because we cannot serve two masters. Only chaste monogamy establishes, advances, and preserves peacemaking plasma with honorable epigenetic effects. Polyamory disqualifies its participants from access to this sacred flux due to complex entanglements with women and children who invariably vie for self-centered favors. Hence, no man can manage polygamy equitably and meet his destiny in peace.

After serious revision of my position on the matter, to my knowledge it appears that Khadijah remained Mohammad's only wife unto her death. No other woman could have taken her place. As discussed in Chapter 4 (Golgotha), she personally assisted his ascent to the sage status of prophethood by means of the rahim grace they collectively gathered for decades. As I said, this doesn't happen overnight or in three days.

Ergo, I posit that chaste monogamy is the bottom-line

apostolic requirement that brings the highest beneficial result. Its conjoined physics and metaphysics can be likened to limbic respirations that regulate the processing of inter-dimensional, inter-penetrating fractals produced in Tesla's unseen plasma, which is likely why deep breathing meditations work. Not the least of these is the pulsating, frequency-dependent, electro-magnetic flux (*EMF*) that couches said ether during the sub-atomic phase transitions of *systems couplings* required to reach the blissful heights of reverent, undulating, sexual intercourse (See: *Sexology For The Wise.* p 237).

Moving on, the metaphysics of eros dynamics known to the ancients is revealing.

> 🗝 EROS MUST BE CONSIDERED AN AUTONOMIC STATE governed directly by the polarity of the sexes in the same way that the presence of positive and negative poles govern everything connected to a magnetic field [called *tsing* in Chinese sexology]. ~ Evola, *Metaphysics of Sex*, p 14

Systems-Coupling literally involves things unseen; which includes the *logos* that is universally and deeply embedded in all of creation with degrees of benefit that are not made accessible to all due to a lack of quality control. But do not mistake this for humanism, pan-theism, or Monism because G-d's word isn't G-d anymore than this book or a song I wrote is me. Such monism is the greatest of religious errors because it makes idolatry mundane.

Our proper enmeshment with *logos* in nature, selves and each other should be the focus of our existence, so that every action and thought will somehow contribute to the sacred fire of its life-preserving hearth. Hence, chaste monogamous fidelity represents the essence of purified intimacy that is required to consciously access and maintain a flow of unadulterated grace for communal benefit, lest impure *EMF*s corrupt the whole. This is a major lesson drawn from NOI's dilemma and Malcolm's death because only chaste monogamy has the correct gravitational flux that properly refracts light on dark matters of deception. This means that when mistakes are made, contrition is the only angle of refraction that provides a solution. There is no other.

mysterium

Evola sussed it years ago; alchemists, poets, and troubadours knew it centuries ago; and all women know it instinctively. Yet unwise pseudo-sapients seek every possible avenue, including the corruption of scripture, to escape monogamy's wise border. In the service of *nafs al-lawwama*, or the pretense of self-criticism that protects evasiveness, they corrupt the penile path. Ancient initiates literally turned *eros* into a holy whore-mongering circus. Presently, they do it for half-time shekels in oversized colosseums for duped slaves whom ~~Jesus~~ called the *walking dead*.

Mr. Poole's mission on behalf of Fard's Ahmadiyya cult was little different. Thinking he had divine right to geriatric prurience, his temple prostitutes comprised "vestal secretaries" whom he serially bedded and abandoned to satisfy his restless, undisciplined *tsing*. This is relevant because long before Noetic Science began ghost-busting superstition, Evola recognized *tsing* as the ever-hungry flux phantom[2] that haunts us precisely where 'bio-resonant *systems-coupling*

---

2. * I call it the 'hungry ghost'. See: **Sexology** https://forum.alginkgo.com/go/NTzOMIeg2i

occurs. Optimal conditions for the proper requital of *tsing's* completely gender-dependent *systems-coupling* necessitates a complementary heterosexual pair positioned in apposite congruent di-valence; meaning a couple whose fundamental *TVC*s complement each other. For Indo-European ancients, *tsing* was the ***mysterium transformationionis*** that, during sacred fertility rites, was said to incarnate the mother goddess (Evola, op.cit.).

Ideally, complementary spouses requite *tsing* regularly because it nurses empyreal certitude by flowing through divinely-lit conduits to fine tune their developmental evolution as mature humans. Such marriages focus on veracious fertility in all realms of human pursuit. But know this, properly requited *tsing* reaches beyond reproduction to navigate every un-jaded path of destiny under countless suns. It is supra-activated *logos*. Properly *tsinged* couples thus stand in apostolic authority because they cooperate with divine forces, which tides determine our *strength-of-desire* to unite with G-d. Indeed, it is a Great Mystery pursued by many but attained by few. Absent the conscious sacrality of *tsing* we make a poor practice of love and politics, which is why fornication is the political norm. But prurience and *gravitas* are poor bedmates.

from the bowels of babil

Each phantom-half of our subliminally desired 'united human being' incessantly seeks communication with its complementary half. It is the core life-drive component that pushes us forward because we cannot attain the teleology of complete maturity if left in unrequited isolation. Then we merely grow old, barren, and unfulfilled. Hence, whatever divides love-birds *en route* to white-haired maturity prevents, represses, or short-circuits the sacred yin-yang of the *tsing mysterium*.

Separating us from this fulfillment defines the *Mystery of Iniquity* as taught by *Harut* & *Marut*. Any of its numerous fixating fetishes maintain prurience and arrest development; add chauvinist mania and you prevent even the semblance of seasoned unity among equitable peers because all becomes drama requiring skilled actors. This is the compounded dilemma Mr Poole brought to American Negroes from the bowels of Babil. It is NOI's cornerstone set on the foundation of Fard's cultured magick. A pox on love.

Like good wine, it takes upwards of sixty-odd years to develop a complete Vitruvian human. But in addition to perversions and false doctrines, impediments to Vitruvian evolution include, forced marriages and multiple consorts—noting that additional lovers complicate rather than improve decision making or optimize resource utilization. To wit:

> 🔑 God sets forth a parable: A man who has for his masters several partners, [all of them] at variance with one another, and a man depending wholly on one person: can these two be deemed equal as regards their condition? Nay, but most of them do not understand this.
>
> ~ M. Asad, Q.39.29

Beginning with children, we discharge our responsibilities within the sacred trust radius of chaste monogamy. This hallowed unicity informs a divinely inscribed social organ of governance as an archetype. Responsible spouses meet *face-to-face* on a continuum, in and out of bed. Their transactional love refracts the intimate conjugal experience our Creator specifically designed to express as unity of purpose after they stop making self-centered impositions on each other. Such peacemaking requires the correct administration of respectively gendered offices via effective communications that establish and maintain a procedural order that defends human dignity for each spouse. When in compliance, they qualify for additional benefits that emanate from unseen realms as a congruent consequence.

Only by personally experiencing the practical advantages of this unity, or by serving those who do, can we reap incremental degrees of *rahim* grace. Conversely, when violating this covenant in the service of those who turn away from chaste fidelity, we reap incremental loss. Thus, Mr. Poole's adultery not only caused his domestic loss of *tsing*, but also a "loss-of-face" for his entire polity, beginning with the understandably inconsolable but honorable Mrs. Poole, who was utterly disheartened on learning of his indiscretions. Hers is NOI's mortified countenance magnified.

By divine design, both genders ideally and equally share decision-making on the conjugal throne of their domicile. Only this peerage preserves 'dignity in unity' as they become 'one flesh', which translates as '*one messenger*' or even '*one body*' when using the biblical archetype. This chair governed Tolkein's *Rivendale,* wherein apposite complemental spouses attended one throne with serene unicity. Such blessed couples consciously choose to responsibly meet the needs of each other and community. If they wax contrary to this purpose, they become the bad-wolf qareen

Contrition

depicted in Dali's *Satan*—only to proudly but blindly wonder about in speculations *beyond their ken*.

> 🔑 For when they became oblivious of Us
> We assigned to them their own evil
> impulses *[speculations]* as their other selves
> *[qareen]*,
> 🔑 And these *[qareen]* made appear goodly
> to them whatever lay open before them
> and whatever was <u>beyond their ken</u>.
>
> ~ M Asad, Q.41.25

It seems Elijah Poole partnered with his *DP*-shadow. He did not lower his gaze or restrain his desire for strange flesh (Q.9.40). What's worse, he made desperate attempts to cage his hungry ghost in a web of dishonor by mistreating helpless women and children who were at his mercy; in contradistinction to Quranic precepts. Had he honestly confessed his need for a younger wife, I suspect the right honorable Mrs Poole would have left his bed (divorce) and soberly helped him find a suitable woman to manage his *tsing*-dynamics. But Poole chose the coward's path and made shameful efforts to escape exposure. After abusing his victims, he then slandered, censored, and countenanced the murder of the right honorable Malcolm-X.

As described by Prof. Naquib Al Attas, *adab* is the clear and precise definition of truth that calls a person, place or thing what it is, in keeping with Al Qur'an's injunction (Q.22.30-32).[3] On discovering his mentor's indiscretions, as NOI's chief spokesman Malcolm-X was ethically obliged to

---

3. The concept of adâb by Syed Muhammad Naquib al-Attas and its

publicly call Mr Poole to account, especially after the old satyr refused contrition in private. Notwithstanding his courage, like Pharaoh's magicians the cost was dear. The game was real.

All things considered, I'm thinking Bumpy Johnson[4] stands in better stead with Allah than does Mr Poole.

---

relevance to education in Indonesia: Ibn Khaldun Journal of Social Science Vol. 1, No. 1, 2019, pp 52-63 DOI: 10.32832/ikjss.v1i1.2385
4. See: Harlem Godfather: The Rap On My Husband, K E Quinones & Mayme Johnson

Dali's Satan

Dalii's Satan James Delingpole: https://forum.alginkgo.com/go/n1DKS4jVxS

13

THE TRUEST RELIGION
A VITRUVIAN MODEL

🔑 *Physical union, taken on its own, is only the mechanism through which is conveyed a process of a higher order, transcending that union and showing it to be part of a whole.*

🔑 *If its transcendental aspect is recognized, mere "pleasure" as a coarse and carnal satisfaction, depending strictly on physiological conditioning, are problematical solutions.*

On Schopenhauer's *Bait For Procreation*

~ Evola, op. cit. p 26

an existential lesson

GOD DID NOT create Adam married to Eve, Suzy, Mark, and at times Madonna, Gaga, or monkeys, dogs, and sheep. Nor did He create a goddess of prostitution devoted to *ars amandi* as did Solon, the great lawgiver; nor did He approve of authorities who watched as queens and vestals had sex with animals or extrajudicial phalli in telestriums, colleges, or coliseums built by *Zeus & Company, Ltd.*, as did Roman, Egyptian, Greek, and Persian potentates and their appointed high priests. In addition to these fondlings, the pious promiscuity of Tibetan tantra has attained naught but chaotic communes such as the Bagwan farce. Only humans hallow indecency and milk the pretense for profitable advantage *pro patria*.

Although monogamous marriage deserves top billing as our core religion, Novalis called its modern cathedral a "*desecrated mystery*". Seventeen hundred years ago St Martin also lamented this grave dishonor:

> 🗝 *If mankind knew what marriage is, it would have, at one and the same time, an extraordinary desire for it and a tremendous fear of it ... for by means of it man could once again be made like God or could end in total ruin.* ~ Evola, op. cit., pp 19, 175

>> 🗝🗝 Because sexual gratification does not wholly requite on its own, we must learn and teach the ongoing art of carefully balancing yin-yang proprieties within the protected estate of chaste conjugal marriage — that is, if we are to realize satisfied love on a continuum. and what's wrong with that? ~ oz

But this approach to fidelity is impossible without the support of a divinely constituted, wholly empathetic community. Moreover, such a confederacy's fidelity must be consciously bound by *The Decalogue*, which, as Jordan

Peterson astutely taught us, is completely reasonable self-evident truth.[1] Without its enforcement, social harmony and communal verve cannot be maintained due to the prurient dissolution that autonomously comes into play by default. A successful polity thus governs solely by embracing the humility of our completely dependent estate. Accept it. It is the existential lesson to be learned for the sixth day of creation's completion; which is yet to happen. I advise you to do whatever you can to make the cut dear reader. (see: Appendices: G-d's Relatives: *a singular note on creation and eschatology*)

Religionists often obviate conjugal sacrality by denigrating *eros* and/or women. Not a few claim that sexuality inherently counteracts divine imminence by transmitting *original sin*; inferring marriage is spiritually inferior to celibacy. To the contrary, when consciously approached, especially with reverence, heterosexual marriage awakens, develops, completes, and supports the maturation of human sacrality because the very act of coitus manifests the divine imminence of a Designer Who delights in our mysterious refractions of His bliss.

Comparatively speaking, ecclesiastical abstinence and sundry other venereal estates are lower planes of existence that often manifest or facilitate dysfunctional imperfections. Such outcomes invariably arrest human development when the unqualified vie for leadership positions. Moreover, some solemnized fetishes are so perverse they directly lead to what St Martin, a Roman Soldier, called "*total ruin*". Pederasty and Catholic Castrati are but traces of this extinction or misdirection of divine grace.

Moreover, because chaste monogamy is holy—*reserved*

---

1. https://forum.alginkgo.com/go/sQbqpsRrgN

for God—we are wise to invoke His name when entering the consecrated temple (*yoni*) to entertain and enjoy the sacral duty of intimate holy communion. Even St Paul called marriage a great mystery with respect to God's relation to the people of Isa (Eph.5) whom he called '*bride of Christ*', much as Hebrews became the bride of Moses. What distracts us from this path of genuine transcendence are differential incidentals that bear the chauvinist cant of interpretive ignorance (Q.48.26).

the grail of *tsing*-bliss

Bi-fold unity within a projected-geometrical state of balanced perfection is attained after years of mutually derived orgasms that literally enlighten the path of reiterative reconciliations that return us as humbly submitted peacekeepers to the sacred source of wisdom. We experience divine love by causing each other to consciously establish its communion, which cleanses and renews us with the waters of reverently placed sexual desire's ecstatic bliss.

When prioritized as a sacred duty, this activity keeps us cleanly on the straight and narrow, in and out of the bedroom, because reiterations require disciplined attention to details that keep romance alive. It's an art form and should never be taken for granted. When carrying afterglows into kitchen and town square, we transcend and transmogrify in complete contradistinction to the call of Mr Poole's unredeemed shadow activities.

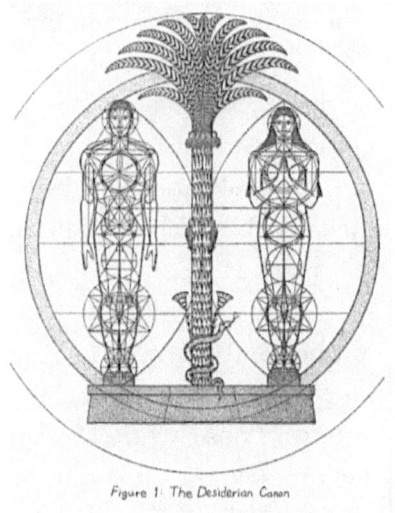

Figure 1: The Desiderian Canon

Apposite not **Opposite**
See: Mysteries of the Vitruvian Man, C Lance Harding,
https://www.scribd.com/document/338006345/The-Man-in-the-Squared-Circle

The road to maturity thus embraces sacred geometry under the royal arch of symmetrical paring; which, when well-matched, humbly crafts a chalice that receives, holds, and distributes the rahim grace of abundance. I'm suspecting this is what Adam somehow lost to shadow long ago. Hence, those who seek sex solely for pleasure are materially fixed and cannot implement metaphysical praxis, except to shamefully curse. Neither can they establish lasting peace because they limit the union to the gratification of base desire, about which Ibn Arabi said:

The sexual act will be a form lacking any spirit.

🔑 Of course, the spirit always remains immanent in the form as such, but it will be imperceptible to him who lies with his wife or with any woman just for sensual pleasure without recognizing Allah as the true object of his desire ... Were he aware, he would also know by virtue of what and whom he enjoys this pleasure, whereby he would become spiritually perfect. [2]

🔑🔑 The right honorable Ibn Arabi suggested that the love of God is the *true object of man's sexual desire.* He is not alone in this assertion. Those who consciously attend the fidelity of *tsing*-dynamics know that our desire for divine bliss compels us to repeatedly revisit sexual ecstasy's continuum. This is not accomplished on any prayer mat unless it is with our spouse; which is to say 'with the appointed loins that authentically refract G-d's love'. Thus, to separate sexual intimacy from heavenly communications is anathema to spiritual perfection; the goal of Harut & Marut protocols, so that divine union goes wanting along with communal unicity, except as *magogites* in the service of *gog*.

This fundamental social priority manifests as follows:

1. the very first thing we wish to learn about anyone is whether or not they are happily situated in a bed of satisfaction with a similarly satisfied spouse. All other constructs regarding community relations, material and not, orbit the answer to this common query, which is why unhappy singles are so sensitive.

---

2. Ibn' Arabi, **Fusus al-hikam** also see **https://quranstruelight.com/**

Unless placed in properly recognized divine order, they remain wild cards whose loyalty is questioned. Until married, and for the sake of communal unicity, they require a form of adoption or sponsorship by a Vitruvian Pair of sages who act as mentors and protectors.

Thus, well-married folks daze and doze in Elysian bliss with the help of well-regulated oxytocin and dopamine titers, protected and enhanced by innumerable unseen spheres of light-filled plasma. It is the divine order spoken of in Al Qur'an.[3] This form of communication confirms supernal immanence by affirming our helpless compulsion to reverently and joyfully conjugate in the presence of a sacred witness.

🗝️🗝️ *I therefore and confidently declare that monogamous marital love is the truest religion.*

Chauvinists and celibates, be ye male or female, take heed. If prior to this reading you did not savvy that monogamous marriage is the divinely protected integrated vessel for ideal human development, you have just been served a writ of divorce from ignorance.

the little death

By furtively satisfying concupiscence, however, as did Mr. Poole, we corrupt *tsing* and invite arrested development. Disordered moral dynamics soon foster individual and

---

3. AS-SALAH is the SOCIAL ORDER based on the DIVINE CODE By Anwar Shaik – Doctor of Education December 2022

communal dissolution by default. When faithfully reverent, over time the undefiled fecundity of chaste *tsing*-dynamics establishes consistent patterns in mind and body that remain in intimate, trinitarian communion. By this means and within this circuit do we pray constantly with good-faith deeds that unerringly seek and find God's will and grace (1Thess.5:17; Esth.6:4).

In a sense, every moment of orgasmic bliss re-immerses us in the formless ocean (*chaos*/plasma) out of which we were created. This mini-nirvana is what classicists call **the little death**. It transpires after we cross the sacred threshold and join our temples, after which the transformative miracles of spiritual growth and maturation spawn and are nourished. If this is so, it is no small wonder that pietists the world over, and with few exceptions, denigrate holy matrimony with an assumed posture of official, spiritual supremacy, which is not only utter nonsense but also supreme arrogance.

The veil that divides Creator from creature is fleetingly tossed aside during the little death's *tsing*-bliss, during which adjustments are made, unseen to seen. Divine union is thereby acknowledged face-to-face and heart-to-heart by spouses with sufficient grit to reverence the sacrality, knowing they hold keys to 'kingdoms within' for each other. Unless betrayed, an ever-present memory of divine love thereafter defines their trinity as the grail that guards its good faith trust. It is the ark that withstands all floods.

The divine aspect of this *mysterium transformationionis* flows from somewhere within Tesla's endless coils of ether to interact with an environment that is subject to genetic and epigenetic variables in contiguous proximity to numerous unseen sources of universal irradiations described in previous chapters. Think long and hard on this, then contemplate Dali's Last Supper once more. The ascendant *Christos* of that imagination is the central theme of humanity's moral striving: which is to attain ascendant one-flesh wholeness in unicity with the will of G-d Almighty: to walk with G-d likeAbraham. It is possible. To abandon this aspiration is to become worse than animals because even they have better sense than to become sub-human, homo-*stupidae*.

mr. poole's prurience

It becomes clear that the fullness of divine communion cannot be had via abstinence, promiscuity, or gender-confused mindsets. Each is devoid of complimentary gender-specific *TVC*-systems-coupling in sync with the sacred geometry of symmetrical apposition. This is because apposite Vitruvian balance requires gender-specific material and epigenetic congruence; phenomena that serial fornicators and adulterers refuse to admit. Like Mr Poole, they mock the divine immanence of chaste monogamy's embrace:

> 🗝 *as he is in that state of concupiscence, it is lust that excites him to do what he does;*

> 🗝 *but as he looks to one woman, and loves to conjoin his life with her life, concupiscence becomes chaste affection, and lust, human love.* [4]

~ E. Swedenborg

---

4. E. Swedenborg, *Conjugal Love*, 448 https://forum.alginkgo.com/go/RVosARFE4R

That transcended lust is love is undiscussed. Its fruit derives from the mature management of *eros*, which discipline and art is perfected in monogamous marriage. Mrs Poole expected this perfectibility from her husband and all spiritually sober folks expect this of their leaders. However, Mr Poole furtively struggled with prurience like a fumbling school boy, even as he approached his seventieth birthday, which attests to his arrested development.

- 🔍 When Clara Muhammad, his wife, the woman who introduced him to master Fard and co-founded NOI became fully aware of her husband's eight children born out of wedlock to different women, she painfully withdrew from an active role in the organization for several years.
    - ▶ Malcolm X then openly accused Elijah Muhammad of immorality.
    - ▶ Similarly, Mirza G Ahmad and his sons also had extra-wives and their inner-circles covered their misgivings. It's no wonder NOI mimes Ahmadiyya, since that is where it learned Islam from.
    - ▶ For years, Muhammad's chief lieutenants at Chicago's Temple No. 2 were able to contain the rumors, at times through fear and intimidation ... some of the women suffered extreme harassment, and were forced to move when explosions occurred next to their shared living quarters. [5]

---

5. SEE: Manning Marable, *Malcolm X : A life of reinvention* https://forum.alginkgo.com/go/Eu-fP22Q5p

Contrition

Many call Poole 'honorable' but withhold the honorific from Malcolm-X; a fact that caught my attention and encouraged this forensic examination all the more. Apologists refuse to discuss Mr. Poole's promiscuity and the cruelty he directed towards the women and children he abused. Like devotee masochists described herein, or like Jesuit-educated Catholics, his pitiful acolytes feel obligated to defend him and divorce infidelity from the supposed greatness of his deeds. Their bias signifies three things: idolatry; criminal collusion; and denial of scripture's warning against adultery.

(Q.24:3-4)

🔑 The adulterer couples with none other than an adulteress — that is, a woman who accords [to her own lust] a place side by side with God;

🔑 And the adulteress couples with none other than an adulterer — that is, a man who accords [to his own lust] a place side by side with God: and this is forbidden unto the believers. Both are equally guilty.

Moreover, Quranic passages that supposedly permit four wives or Mohammad's polyamory do no such thing.

🔑 Contrary to early Jewish biographer's insinuations about the family life of Mohammad, we have plenty of Quranic testimonies to believe that he could never have allowed or indulged in polygamy. The Quran never addressed the "Wives" of the holy Messenger whenever it uses the words "Azwaaj-un-Nabi / Nisaa'un-Nabi". [6]

pharaoh's error

As God-incarnate and messiah, Fard and his messenger would have known all the above and that reality was designed as an interactive system of mutual exchange, all of which hold specific consequences. The tally so far: Louis Farrakhan has twenty-two children, and Elijah Poole, twenty-five from nine different women we know of. If that makes you envious, you automatically disqualify for the rahim grace under discussion.

I have ten children by four wives whom I serially married and divorced. I do not repent of the children but rather of the foolish journey that led me to think such chauvinist arrogance was justifiable. Fard's litter has thus far escaped notice because his history has been carefully expunged. According to Dr Fanusie, Fard continued to secretly instruct Mr Poole after quietly returning to America from temporary occultation in Fiji (see Appendices: Investigators). Brother Warith did an excellent job with his whitewash and has been likened to Billy Graham for bringing American Negroes a better shade of Islam. Kudos. Nonetheless, I suspect his careful watch over NOI's collapse is comparable to burning the libraries of Constantinople and Alexandria, both of which held documents that

---

[6]. Presenting The Quran in its Own Words By Aurangzaib Yousufzai https://forum.alginkgo.com/go/xHLleKObEk // Rebuttal of Fictitious Traditional Interpretations

also see: A Sherazi, # 41: Four wives: crime against the Quran, Quranic Research Inc. https://forum.alginkgo.com/go/ECnsGz8MDe

Contrition

would otherwise have destroyed any hope of Vatican legitimacy. There is indeed a parallel.

Digging deeper into mystery religion initiations that misled Alexander, with the help of faithful scholars we find that the doctrinal inventiveness of NOI's *"morally corrupt founder"* was part of a carefully planned infiltration that distinctly led folks away from the Vitruvian model. Mr Fard was likely a devotee of the Ahmadiyya Cult, whose founder, Mirza Ghulam Ahmad, was famous for inculcating salacious behavior, even incest. But why did we have to wait until 2014 for a Georgetown Thesis written by Prof. Fatima Fanusie to tell us? (see Appendices: Investigators).

NOI's well-disciplined acolytes couched the greed and lust of Fard & Poole Ltd. with masterful apologetics while nursing a group identity crisis. Stupefied, they looked past Poole's violation of several wombs whose fruit should be honored as a source of renewed hope. Where is honor or sacrality in this? They cut several curious corners with feeble natterings that waxed as ritual murder. Then, thinking they did G-d worthy service, NOI lowlifes covered his crimes like furtive Jews for decades, an odd but nevertheless common form of spiritual blindness. I ask 'where was the wifely restraint that should have halted the recidivism of these hoodlums'? Where was the common sense auntie with a rollin pin ready to strike the wayward head? Among all those sister robed saints I saw no yin balancer in view, except for Wakanda screenings. Shameful.

Anything other than heart felt contrition for these collective crimes expresses arrogant denial—which is the primal error of Pharaoh. Denial compounds the perfidy and only temporarily protects those who've misplaced their trust and loyalty. Even so, perhaps this cloak's pious veneer is the lesser evil? But evil it is.

Let those with ears hear this peal before the final bell is rung.

14

LIFE AT THE BOTTOM
A CHASTE CONDUIT

🗝 Every man is born corporeal, becomes sensual, then natural, and successively rational, and if he does not stop there, he becomes spiritual.

~ *E. Swedenborg*

I cannot sufficiently express my admiration for Mr Swedenborg. Please take the time to consult his library. Like Goethe, he had no peer.

hushed injustice

Conjugal fidelity invites, builds, and preserves institutional unity because it is The Great Mystery's divinely approved unicity consort. There is no substitute or comparative analogue that so effectively incarnates divine guidance with such protean protection. Indeed, balanced masculine-to-feminine harmony optimizes the path to conscious maturity. If you do not see such couples in position of authority it is because democracy serves the majority interest in compounded ignorance, which is readily marshaled by *DP*-elitists who specialize in neuro-politics.

As a tangential correlate, women should dress modestly because immodest dress invites and promotes prurience. Women should never ever share their charms with strangers, lest they become accomplices to unrighteous dissolution. This discernment separates us from the animal kingdom. It makes us human, but only when sapiently held as precious. Thus, modesty rules the Kingdom of G-d so that immodesty cannot be tolerated in the least, because it is a slippery slope to the oubliette of no return.

The subversion of such a high cultural goal occurs when charismatics dress *pseudo*-science as fact and *speculative* doctrines as truth. Because there was no censor to warn Negroes at the bottom against charlatans like *Fard & Poole Ltd.*, both *DP*-opportunists partnered and flourished. Thus, NOI ascendency flew into brass heavens only to refract absurd fancies and flat earth lizard people who hold Andromeda's Superman in high esteem: a page taken out of the Sabbatean Pleiades Myth for Dogon Wakanda lovers. Such fanciful noise enjoys generous apologetics (Matt.12:43-45) that cover gross errors. For example, calling cosmology's dark matter *'black matter or melanin'*. I heard this proudly broadcast as scientific fact in 2024 by a preeminent student of Warith Mohammad.

But I'm guessing the universe cares nothing for what we think. We all receive its sunshine, water, and ants. Clean pressed suits in neat ghettoes with swept streets and gutters do not define divine guidance or the dispensation of *Rahim* grace. Surely they help, but even Wall Street's evil mongers dress well and keep clean streets. So think again because long after hushed injustice hits our history books as a success story, those who maintain well-heeled traps for its poseurs will fail the test on Judgement Day. Good lord! Even communist communitarians know they cannot maintain peaceful domains when swag and booty are openly on the table. NOI's god-men were no different. To wit:

- 🔍 As with other sectors of the NOI body, the financial empire was tied tightly to the Messenger personally. Wallace Muhammad wrote:
  - 🔍🔎 No one knew the condition of the business because no accounting systems were in effect to monitor national income and expenditures ... the economic health of the Nation of Islam is not what it was projected to be. Long-term debt commitments had financed large-scale projects, putting strains on obligatory donations and draining other financial enterprises of their profit. [1]

The root of this shame rests in denying the loss of divine approval and *self*-esteem over the entire affair. To cover this nakedness, apologists either replace or modify the chaotic rumination of *Life At The Bottom*, with or towards a lesser evil.[2]

Chastity is an especial conduit that receives the purist of

---

1. M Gardell, **Countdown to Armageddon**, p.14. https://www.goodreads.com/book/show/927867-countdown-to-armageddon
2. **Life at The Bottom** https://www.goodreads.com/book/show/117161.Life_at_the_Bottom

grace treasures. Caste adrift on planet earth, it is our lifeline. When grateful for gifts of life we please G-d as faithful lovers who practice the complementary balance that earns and perfects fidelity's grace-filled grail of unicity. Your spouse ideally delights eye, heart, and groin, and when taken together the yin/yang total amounts to more than your individual sums. This exchange of chaste fidelity between spouses holds the collective more worthy than the individual, it creates a trust that turns respectively gendered spheres of influence towards heaven as a valued collective, so that together they accomplish iterations of intimate *face-to-face* encounters on a continuum, ideally within the context of a supportive community.

If you cannot house such thoughts with reverence, you are likely reprobate or with the wrong mate, or know not *how* or *who* to love. So be warned and know that all couplings that entertain immodesty alter the compass and turn subsequent events towards mischief, disharmony, suffering, and loss—noting that degrees of fornication begin with imagination and inevitably lead to degrees of spiritual adultery, and to St Martin's ruin.

I suspect NOI testosterone storms took their boardrooms with the same goatish tempestuousness that forever prevents Negro or Arab unity. Its bells of chauvinist ruination ring hellish consequences in vast empty stretches of vainly imagined, inter-galactic melanin. Consider why Cain killed Abel and you begin to discern urbane versus rural mindsets as 'materialist tyrant' versus 'obedient servant'. You will see the organized barbarity of Rome versus those who navigate Sea, Steppe, or Mountain in relative peace. There you will discover the pretense of a superior-minded gentility that masks evil intent with finesse, crosses all boundaries, and quickly murders whistleblowers like the honorable Malcolm-X. It is the Mystery of Iniquity that rules over Sin (Gen.4.7).

sultans of swag & booty

Sadly, what follows describes the sad state of arrested development that owned Elijah Poole at seventy years of age.

🗝 *Unruly prurience blindly causes the following:*

- ⚑ not only weakness and consequent wants, but also
- ⚑ impurities and immodesties are occasioned,
- ⚑ by reason of which conjugal love — the jewel of human life — cannot be perceived and felt in its purity and chastity, and thus neither in its sweetness and the delights of its prime;
- ⚑ not to mention the mischiefs occasioned to both the body and the mind,
- ⚑ and also the disavowed allurements that deprives conjugal love of its blessed delights and turns it into loathing...
- ⚑ immoderate and inordinate fornications are like burning flames which, arising out of ultimates,
- ⚑ consume the body, parch the fibres, defile the blood, and vitiate the rational principles of the mind;
- ⚑ for they burst forth like a fire from the foundation into the house, which consumes the whole. ...

🗝 *To prevent these mischiefs is the duty of parents;*

> *for a grown-up youth, inflamed with lust, cannot as yet from reason impose restraint upon himself.*
> [3]
>
> E Swedenborg

Ladies and Gentlemen, to abandon marital fidelity and its attendance to modesty is to open the gates of hell. Had NOI been guided and guarded by agents of truth, their leaders would have fearfully kept the tenet. Sadly, neither Fard or Poole earned the right honorable badge of fidelity that marks every sage. Hence, their claims to saintly, *wahy-*inspiration status are entirely bogus.

What Mr. Swedenborg described three-hundred years ago defines the term 'infidel', per scripture, and as instilled in our collective psyche (*fitrah*). The word qualifies anyone who induces the curse of inverse outcomes per divine law. Such cursing inescapably comes into play when lies and liars are permitted to enjoy purloined booty and fallacious celebrity. I could cite pages of proofs and weeks of pious drivel proving that NOI sultans of swag and booty were never humble servants of *The Great Mystery*. To the contrary, they did their very best to heap *darkness upon darkness* (Q.24:40).

the emporium

In closing I paraphrase the cult's profile using Jordan Peterson's template for practiced sociopaths:

---

3. https://swedenborg.com

Contrition

🗝 The society built by NOI's god-man and false messiah is a temple of sadomasochism. Susceptible masochists climb its thousand-and-one-stairs only to reach a bizarre worldview that stabilizes the cultural magick of paranoia. Its religio-neuro-political conditioning allowed Fard & Poole to dominate distressed victims who suffered the misplacement of trust.

🗝🗝 They built an emporium for predators whose gang of mountebanks refilled failed fortunes by dancing a mesmerizing jig that compounded ignorance. They spewed tall tales with false histories that couched imaginary worlds of remiss commotion. They spread a canopy of risk-free tyranny, under which rot sold and the beauty of truth failed to receive its rightful throne: that of chaste fidelity. [4]

Life's existential grail is the chaste fidelity of monogamous marriage for which chauvinist misguidance is anathema. Emanuel Swedenborg and the reprobate Evola both agree that giving robust honorifics to dead womanizing liars and murderers is anathema to genuine cosmopolitanism. Indeed, NOI preserved and elaborated myths of misguidance taught by Speculative Freemasons under the sway of *B'nai B'rith* Kabbalists and capitalists whose platforms were constructed by Harut & Marut.

Jesuits revised them a few hundred years ago and have since sedulously encroached every decision making chair on the planet where they pull strings from behind curtains at the end of every yellow brick road. These strings are attached to Dionysian mystery initiations at the capstone, which require intoxicated boys to bed a handful of mature

---

4. for dissertation see: https://forum.alginkgo.com/go/8WkEa0Cp8Y

women in a one night stand at the feet of an Isis mock-up. These big-brother leaders answer to hidden auspices and masters who seek tyranny by enslaving or destroying all 'others'.

Spawn of this Mystery of Iniquity, NOI had the rudimentary appearance and functions of a virile and cohesive group-feeling. Albeit, they misused the genuine Islamic *esprit de corps* that Ibn Khaldun and others say Muslims lost to Persian Magi long ago (See Appendices: Islam's Subversion). NOI could have taken jaded irritants, walled them off via the Noetic Science of *adab*, and then turned them into pearls. But magical thinkers forever cling to fabrications and then fiercely deny evidence that contradicts their aberrant worldview.

The world does not exchange magical thinking for operative skills that deliver justice. Neither does heaven accept such leadership. Anyone who deems poseurs honorable must own this truth and submit to honest humiliation —as did brother Malcolm, the contrite. So take care you are not undertaken: snapped up and swallowed, then delivered to the final oubliette, assimilated by the force of stupidity.

If this shoe fits, repent and patiently suffer the apoplectic seizure of its painful remorse, and do so in anticipation of prodigal restitution. Many will fail to comprehend the admonishment, but those who practice the learned art of *adab* will, like heaven, mark all who reject contrition because they know G-d's favor conditionally attends the Holy Grail of chaste monogamy. It is written. Be comforted.

Contrition

MAY our Source Creator allow the memory and legatees of the Right Honorable Malcolm-X to prosper and be granted due diligence, here and hereafter. May this justice refract clear waters for troubled souls and guide them to honor its chaste conduit.

omar zaid,
Christmas 2024, Liberty Ky.

Afterword

🗝 *"Such a colonization of negritoes,* (paraphrased)*: represents the apex of moral degradation in which vanity can find no rest because it is without apposite resonance.*

Celine

APPENDICES

God's Relatives
Investigators, References
Ibn Maymun's Protocols
On Polygamy
Psychopath Profile
Islam's Subversion
The Khazar Conversion
Annunaki
Zionism

⚖ G-d's Relatives

G-D's FIRST-DEGREE RELATIVES
per biblical allegory/metaphor

1. "*Israel is my son* : say to Pharaoh, 'This is what the LORD says: "*Israel is my firstborn son*" (Exodus 4:22)

   This phrase refers of anyone or any group of believers who reflect the Light of Genesis called = *Significant Luminary*. They incarnate the word of God = *logos* made flesh). Jesus and his mother were among the purest examples of homo-sapient *logos* thus far incarnate from the pre-primordial reserve.

2. *Kenan was the son of Enosh. Enosh was the son of Seth. Seth was the son of Adam. Adam was the son of God. When Israel was a child, then I loved him and called my son out of Egypt. (Hosea 11:1)*
3. He said to me, 'Your son, Solomon, is the one who shall build My house and My courts; for *I*

have chosen him to be a son to Me, and I will be a father to him. (1 Chronicle 28:6)
4. *He who overcomes* will inherit these things, and I will be his God and *he will be My son*. (Rev 21:7)
5. Now there was a day when the *sons of God* came to present themselves before the LORD, and Satan also came among them. (Job 1:6)
6. *Bene Elohim means 'Sons of God'*
7. *Luke called Adam the Son of God (Lk 3:38);*
8. He that walketh in the darkness knoweth not whither he goeth. While ye have the light, believe in the light, that ye may be *sons of light*. (John 12:35–36). Hence: <u>*son-of G-d* is equivalent to *son-of light.*</u>
9. As many as received him, to them gave he the power *to become sons of God.* (John 1:12–13).
10. <u>Sons and *daughters of men*</u> are followers of said prophets and prophetesses: He that soweth good seed is the *son of man* (of truth); the field is the world, and the seed is sons and daughters of the kingdom. (Matt.13:37–38)
11. There are indications that a Yemeni Jewish sect called *Ezra*, was also referred to as a 'Son of God'.

All is metaphor. The Quran states that all such persons were his servants (Q21.26-27). Thus, biblical kinship = divine service ...

a singular note on creation and eschatology

It is worth noting here that, contrary to the modern Darwinian Theory of Evolution with its controversial 'missing links', the Creation of **Adam**, or human species, has been emphasized in Quran, in very clear terms, as an absolutely separate, new and independent Creative Stage, distinct and superior from all other forms of life existing prior to its inception or establishment. It is also a foregone conclusion that, contrary to the mythical tales coming to us about this theme through traditional interpretations from all Scriptures, the progressive minds among us have already started perceiving and acknowledging that **Adam** was not the name of a particular individual who was allegedly molded or sculpted from wet, soft mud into the present shape of man and then blown life into by infusing God's spirit into his body. Excepting some retarded minds, or blind conformists still entangled in myths, the modern conscious man knows for certain that the name **Adam simply represents** the human species.

This completely new species was launched as the FIFTH STAGE of creative process. It can be named as "Fifth" because we can clearly witness four major earlier stages of creation, or life, flawlessly functioning before us within their closed circles or systems. These are: the Cosmic Stage, the stage of Planet Earth with its formation of physical Laws, the Vegetative Stage and the Animal Stage. It is widely known now, and the Quran and earlier Scriptures confirm this fact, that the act of creation was designed in Six successive Stages (Sittati Ayyaam – Six days - ستّة ايّام). Five of those stages have been launched one after the other up till the present time, and are doubtlessly observed functioning within their fixed parameters. While the Sixth and Final Stage is promised to attain its "phenomenal launch or establishment" (Al-Qiyamah – القيامة، قيام، قام) in some unknown distant future, and is given the name of the Hereafter in the Quran and the earlier Divine Scriptures.

https://forum.alginkgo.com/go/5Obn8RgVno

⚖ Investigators, References

1. **Finding WD FARD, John Andrew Morrow (2019)**

https://www.cambridgescholars.com/product/978-1-5275-2199-5

2. **AK Arian (2017). Chameleon: The True Story of WD Fard**

https://forum.alginkgo.com/go/7d8K-6uCXC

3. *Malcolm, is the true messiah,* he transcended them all, NOI, FBI, and even Rome. He began to expose them all as agents of the Mystery of Iniquity. This is why he was murdered.
   - 🔍 *JE Hoover was deathly afraid of Malcolm-X" ... puppets managed by puppeteers, who themselves were hewn from the Mystery. Malcolm indicted Poole for nepotism and senility ... moreover, Poole did not walk the talk for black civil rights (ARM)*

♎︎ Investigators, References

~ Abdul Rahman Mohammad (ARM):

https://www.instagram.com/arm.legacy/?hl=en // https://www.abdur-rahman muhammad.com/about-1

4. **March 26, 2014.** THE LEGACY OF FARD MUHAMMAD, founder of the Lost Found Nation of Islam, has perplexed scholars of the Nation of Islam and Islamic development in Twentieth Century America. **Fatima Fanusie** approached the understudied intellectual heritage and missionary activism of the Lahore heirs of Ghulam Ahmad's Ahmadiyya movement as the critical link to understanding Fard Muhammad and the Nation of Islam in America.
   - 🔍 **The dominant Islamic missionary group operating in America at the time of the development of the Nation of Islam was the Ahmadiyya movement.**
     - Between 1888 and 1975 Ahmadiyya intellectuals conceived of and implemented multi pronged strategies for affecting American religious development and cultivating Islam in American society. Dr. Fanusie argues that **the Nation of Islam was but one aspect of strategic Ahmadiyya efforts** to cultivate Islam in America.

   https://icjs.org/people/fatimah-fanusie/

♎ Investigators, References

5. **BARBERSHOP CONVERSATIONS** NEW FILM: *9 WIVES*,

https://www.youtube.com/watch?v=TzxtrfgVff0*

6. **Malcolm X's Daughter Ilyasah Shabazz** on Her Father's Legacy & the New Series "Who Killed Malcolm X?"

https://www.youtube.com/watch?v=IyzEv7XM2bY

7. **Malcolm-X Condemns Elijah Mohammad**

https://forum.alginkgo.com/go/sCfLD8S7h3

☪ Ibn Maymun's Protocols

Abdullah ibn Maymun's Protocols

There are nine steps in all. These four are major:

1. to link together into one body the vanquished and the conquerors;
2. to unite in the form of a vast secret society with many degrees of initiation: 1) free-thinkers who regarded religion only as curb for the people, and 2) bigots of all sects;
3. to make tools of believers in order to give power to skeptics; to induce conquerors to overturn the empires they had founded;
4. to build up a party, numerous, compact, and disciplined, which in due time would give the throne, if not to himself, at least to his descendants.

Reinhart Dozy, *Spanish Islam*, Eng. trans., pp. 404

They proceeded to the admission and initiation of new proselytes only by degrees and with great reserve; for, as the sect had at the same time a political object and ambitions, its interest was above all to have a great number of partisans in all places and in all classes of society. It was necessary therefore to suit themselves to the character, the temperament, and the prejudices of the greater number; what one revealed to some would have revolted others and alienated for ever spirits less bold and consciences more easily alarmed.

Silvestre de Sacy, *Mémoires sur la Dynastie des Assassins*, Vol. IV. (1818).

⚖ On Polygamy

From Brother Sherazi
https://quranicresearch.com/

The present Islamic literatures and all the translators of the Quran corrupted the translation of the only verse 4:3 providing the justification for the four wives to male Muslim believers. Their corrupt translations have provided the open license for religious prostitution by male Muslim believers. The rich Muslims oligarchs specially, from the Middle East have established their harms (dens of religious prostitution) the world over by marrying young, poor girls. Economic servitude is the main reason for this sexual slavery and social injustice. In the Philippines the poor girls are forced to involve themselves in prostitution.

In verse 4;3 the Quran gives the details about the measures for the improvement of the economical condition of weak segments of the society or community. It provides details on how to handle the economical crisis of weak segments of the society.

☪ On Polygamy

Q.4:1

يَـٰٓأَيُّهَا ٱلنَّاسُ ٱتَّقُوا۟ رَبَّكُمُ ٱلَّذِى خَلَقَكُم مِّن نَّفْسٍ وَٰحِدَةٍ وَخَلَقَ مِنْهَا زَوْجَهَا وَبَثَّ مِنْهُمَا رِجَالًا كَثِيرًا وَنِسَآءً ۚ وَٱتَّقُوا۟ ٱللَّهَ ٱلَّذِى تَسَآءَلُونَ بِهِۦ وَٱلْأَرْحَامَ ۚ إِنَّ ٱللَّهَ كَانَ عَلَيْكُمْ رَقِيبًا

O mankind! reverence your Guardian-Lord, who created you from a single person, created, of like nature, His mate, and from them twain scattered (like seeds) countless men and women;- reverence Allah, through whom ye demand your mutual (rights), and (reverence) the wombs (That bore you): for Allah ever watches over you. ~
Yusuf Ali

A More Faithful Translation

🗝 *Caution to those who cherish humanity, or those who harbor a deep yearning for peace in their minds* يا أَيُّهَا النّاسُ

🗝 *Adhere to the laws of* اتَّقُوا *your Nourisher* رَبَّكُمْ *He who has ordained the very measures for you* خَلَقَكُم *from the unique measures of the Quran* مِن نَفْسٍ واحِدَةٍ *and has shaped the foundation* وَخَلَقَ مِنها *for living in harmony or working together in fellowship* زَوجَها *and disseminated* وَبَثَّ *countless* كَثيرًا *strong* رِجالٌ *and weak traits* وَنِساءً

🗝 *Therefore, uphold the laws of Allah* وَاتَّقُوا اللَّهَ *through whom you seek your mutual rights (economic, justice, and social rights)* الَّذي تَساءَلونَ بِهِ *and strive to create nurturing conditions for growth and flourishing (just as the mother's*

☪ On Polygamy

womb and the earth's embrace sustain life) وَالأرحَام Verily, Allah's laws are ever vigilant over you (like the watchfulness of a commanding general) إِنَّ اللَّهَ كَانَ عَلَيْكُمْ رَقِيبًا

Q.4:2

وَءَاتُوا۟ ٱلْيَتَـٰمَىٰٓ أَمْوَٰلَهُمْ ۖ وَلَا تَتَبَدَّلُوا۟ ٱلْخَبِيثَ بِٱلطَّيِّبِ ۖ وَلَا تَأْكُلُوٓا۟ أَمْوَٰلَهُمْ إِلَىٰٓ أَمْوَٰلِكُمْ ۚ إِنَّهُۥ كَانَ حُوبًا كَبِيرًا

> To orphans restore their property (When they reach their age), nor substitute (your) worthless things for (their) good ones; and devour not their substance (by mixing it up) with your own. For this is indeed a great sin. ~ Yusuf Ali:

A More Faithful Translation

- 🗝 And administer or handle وَأَتُوا financial matters in the right way أَموَالَهُم for the economically destitute, those living in hunger, grief, and sorrow (the segment of society) الْيَتَامَى.
- 🗝 And do not substitute your worthless possessions or policies for their good ones, nor exchange good policies for corrupt ones وَلَا تَتَبَدَّلُوا الْخَبِيثَ بِالطَّيِّبِ
- 🗝 And do not manipulate laws or authority to dominate or consume وَلَا تَأْكُلُوا their belongings or property along with your own possessions أَموَالَهُم إِلَى أَموَالِكُم.
- 🗝 Indeed, this will lead society into a profound crises of pain and sorrow. إِنَّهُ كَانَ حُوبًا كَبِيرًا

☪ On Polygamy

Q.4:3

وَإِنْ خِفْتُمْ أَلَّا تُقْسِطُوا۟ فِى ٱلْيَتَٰمَىٰ فَٱنكِحُوا۟ مَا طَابَ لَكُم مِّنَ ٱلنِّسَآءِ مَثْنَىٰ وَثُلَٰثَ وَرُبَٰعَ ۖ فَإِنْ خِفْتُمْ أَلَّا تَعْدِلُوا۟ فَوَٰحِدَةً أَوْ مَا مَلَكَتْ أَيْمَٰنُكُمْ ۚ ذَٰلِكَ أَدْنَىٰ أَلَّا تَعُولُوا۟

> If ye fear that ye shall not be able to deal justly with the orphans, Marry women of your choice, Two or three or four; but if ye fear that ye shall not be able to deal justly (with them), then only one, or (a captive) that your right hands possess, that will be more suitable, to prevent you from doing injustice. ~ Yusuf Ali:

A More Faithful Translation

> 🔑 And if you are concerned وَإِنْ خِفْتُم that you may not be able to ensure economic justice أَلَّا تُقْسِطُوا۟ with the vulnerable community فِي ٱلْيَتَٰمَىٰ, then in this case, you may form associations or enter into relationships with what seems appropriate to you فَٱنكِحُوا۟ مَا طَابَ لَكُم for the vulnerable segment of society مِنَ ٱلنِّسَآءِ;
>
> 🔑 You may take on the economic responsibility of two, three, or four مَثْنَىٰ وَثُلَٰثَ وَرُبَٰعَ. But if you still have concerns that you may not be able to uphold justice فَإِنْ خِفْتُمْ أَلَّا تَعْدِلُوا۟, then remain, isolate yourself تَعْدِلُوا۟ فَوَٰحِدَةً or maintain responsibility only for those already under your care أَوْ مَا مَلَكَتْ أَيْمَٰنُكُمْ, as this will be more appropriate and will prevent undue economic burden ذَٰلِكَ أَدْنَىٰ أَلَّا تَعُولُوا۟.

⚭ On Polygamy

NB: In Arabic, Kajteja signifies a woman who delivers an immature baby.

see also: https://forum.alginkgo.com/go/
ECnsGz8MDe

⚖ Psychopath Profile

Regarding Hypocrites: They

- view us from a certain distance, like a parallel species.
- do not experience love for people they are related to or friendly with ... are virtually unfamiliar with the enduring emotions of love for another person, particularly the marriage partner; it constitutes a fairytale
- they are so brazen about what they say and do that it sounds truthful even when it isn't
- PPP's have an amazing facility for lying. They can spin plausible sounding narratives and lies in the moment, when most people would stammer or struggle. They even have the "ability and willingness to weave a web of lies that can reach over years.

      - the level of untruthfulness is really breathtaking in dark personality
      - people of DP consciously and deliberately exploit, mislead, and manipulate extensively and frequently.
      - This includes complex maneuvering, telling different people conflicting narratives,
      - ensuring these people are kept apart or do not believe the credibility of the other so the truth is not exposed.
      - They compel people to believe things where there is evidence to the contrary and do things they would not usually do

- the subtle and relentless grooming of everyone around them to believe in the created public persona: 'upstanding citizen,' 'well respected,' 'he is above reproach,' etc.
- higher functioning people of DP are likely to secure media or public attention for their acts of 'goodwill' e.g. They can champion children's safety while raping kids at the same time.
- Those who see only the DP façade increasingly try to defend them, believing they are being unfairly treated.
- there are multiple personas, each one is entirely different, and all are completely contrived … each persona may include gestures, dress, facial expressions, vocabulary choice, and accents.
- easily switch between personas.
- each "personality" is a tool created in order to manipulate particular people

- do not engage in manipulation of the victim directly, they engage in manipulating someone else to damage the victim and the manipulated person will have no idea they are in fact harming the victim, thinking they are doing a good thing
- some PPP's don't feel the need to adopt personas. For instance, highly placed PPP's may feel they can just rely on their "seniority or position."
- do not take ownership for their role in causing harm, suffering, and/or distress in others

SEE: H Koehli Psychopaths: Masks of Sanity

Psychopath Profile

They shunt away evidence to the contrary while proudly and militantly wearing pathocratic garments that mark an infantile resistance to truth (defiant petulance) that belies a complete lack of self-trust. This translates as a pervasive paranoia, which root is an incomplete identity as human. Since the latter requires chaste marriage, betrayal is to be expected when dealing with a *DP* persona. For them, criminality is innate. They also lack insight because they cannot learn from experience. Thus, their epigenetic inputs become enmeshed as ponerogenesis.

David Abramowitz

Psychopath Profile

Persistent Predatory Personality (PPP) Model

Attributes (20)

Group 1: They drive the agenda
1. A drive for control, power, dominance
2. Self-view of superior and special, entitled
3. A pathological, explosive inner response to being compromised or challenged
4. Vengeful
5. Uncompromising

Group 2: They are motivated and operate differently and darkly
6. Predatory (including exploitative)
7. Sadistic and cruel
8. Has a low regard for laws, regulations, and agreements, as well as social and moral codes
9. Sexual/relationship boundarylessness
10. Unreasonable expectations of others

Group 3: The truth is not easy to distinguish or believe
11. Actively cultivates façade of 'normal'
12. Chameleon-like
13. Dishonest
14. Devious and manipulative (including calculated) and involving consciously misleading others to be inadvertently complicit. The DP superpower!
15. Unwillingness to accept responsibility for negative impacts they cause

Group 4: They don't experience feelings in the same way as others
16. Without authentic emotion (emotional responses are acted)
17. Callous
18. Unremorseful
19. Self-interested
20. Brazen

⚖ Islam's Subversion

AASATANA:
A Synoptic History of Islam's Subversion

by the late Aurangzaib
Yusufzai

As described earlier in this writing, in 656 C.E., immediately following the martyrdom of Caliph Uthmaan, the "Al- Hukm", viz., the Divine Kingdom was subjected to unrest and turbulence. With the assassination of Caliph Ali in 661, it was completed. The local Jewish element was fully involved in complicity in the murder of Caliphs Uthmaan and Ali. It should be made evident here that, after having been defeated in the battles of Ahzaab and Khayber etc, the sizable population of Jews settled in the Arabian Peninsula:

- 1-600,000 migrated from Iraq in 578 C.E. during the reign of Hormuzd IV – Ref. " UMMAT KA BOHRAAN" by Asraar Alam, Dar-al-Ilm, New Delhi, 2nd ed. Feb.2006.
- also consider southern Arabia where arabs had become Jews. Ref: Maxime Rodinson, ISRAEL: A COLONIAL SETTLER STATE?, New York, 1973, pp.79,80.)

Although rendered unworthy of armed confrontation, Jews had changed their tactics and organized underground. A substantial number of highly educated Jews had deceptively converted to Islam, and in the garb of Muslim Scholars, had started their versatile and multi-dimensional conspiracy of adulterating the Quran's Divine philosophy.

Through this change of tactics, they had succeeded in reaching the highest circles of the ruling class within the next few years. In this respect, two prominent Jewish Scholars' names are part of our History who attended the supreme consultative body (Senate) of Caliph Umar, **Ka"ab Ahbaar** and **Sabaa bin Shamoun**. They also had the backing of Rome's Christian Government, represented by their highly influential emissary, **Jafeenat-al-Khalil.** This man lived in Madina and had held top positions in the Christian Arab Government of Heerah, in the north of Arabia, a satellite state under the Byzantine Empire.

Defeated elements of Persian Magii also participated in this unholy alliance. In short, as Amir Mu'aawiyah bin Abi Safyan refused to recognize the legitimacy of Caliph Ali's Government and proclaimed his autonomy, inevitably demolishing "Al-HUKM" to break the Ummat's unity. This afforded full opportunity for Crypto Jewish Scholars to implement their plans.

As soon as Bani Umayyad"'s forceful domination devastated the true spirit of Divine Rule, the first target of the Jewish conspiracy was achieved. They then set out to vehemently achieve the other remaining targets. It is likely that by 130-140 C.E. the Quran's Jewish interpretations (Tafaseer) and Seerat-e-Rusool by Maghaazi, were compiled and began spreading throughout the Muslim World.

Founding pillars of this stage include historic names like *Ibn-e-Shahab Zohri* (d.124 AH), *Mohammad ibn-e-Ishaaq Yasaar* (d.151 AH), the original author of *Seerat-e-Ibn-e-Hishaam*, and *Mohammad bin As-Saaib Kalabi* (d.146 AH), author of *Tafseer-e-Ibn-e-Abbas*, and others. In another hundred years, i.e., by 850 C.E. these Crypto Jewish Scholars had raised an entire generation of scholars and Sufis within Muslim intelligentsia. They were never to deviate from this fabricated "Religion of Islam" at any cost.

By 900 C.E. this college no longer needed to stay on, and most set sails and departed. From then on the same tafaseer overwhelmingly predominant without interruption, as the result of hard work done by malicious Jewish interpreters. This fact is amply proved by the heavy influx into Quranic interpretations of material from the narrations of the Old Testament (Tauraat). Hadith also, often describing the Shaan-e-Nuzool factor of Quranic verses, is full of stories from the Jewish tradition.

The IMAMAT theory, on which rest the foundations of Shiism were laid by the famous Jewish scholar, **Sabaa" bin Shamoun** (and his son **Abdallah ibn-e- Sabaa**), for whom many prominent religious scholars have called Shi"ites, "Sabaa"is".

At long last, over the past one-hundred-and-fifty years, as a result of an awakening infused by various freedom movements, some scholars concentrated on compiling fresh translations of Al Quran with realistic exegesis. Gradually, the true face of Divine philosophy began to manifest in the dark oblivion. This turn of events threatens the long term plans of old Jewish infiltrators and their successors, the "Muslim Clergy" and "Sufis", whose segments and their establishments find themselves in the state of a turmoil. They stand prepared to defend and preserve of the age-old sectarian and ritualistic philosophies.

Their most recent plan was to prepare and publish, on a global scale, some 21 different versions (Qir"ats/Ahraf) of Quranic text under the sponsorship and support of oppressive Arab regimes who aimed to keep the Quran corrupt and controversial; an ancient legacy contrived by Pagan Arabs of the Bani Umayyad in league with the Jewish elders of the time. all outer parameters indicate that present Jewish elders are watching closely the perceptible end of their old tactical plans.

Presently, the Illuminati have a new strategy of defiance. Signs suggest that, along with contaminating our "religious institutions", Zionist influences are infiltrating the purely Quranic establishments also. Seeing the end of the spell once cast, of the religionalization of Divine Philosophy these last 1400 years, foreign powers now have a new plan of subversion. I call it the "materialization of Divine Philosophy", which means interpreting Quranic texts with a purely materialistic oriented secular perspective and terms.

For this purpose, a plan is envisaged whereby Quran is

♈ Islam's Subversion

to be declared the output of the intellect of a genius person, and a secularist exegesis is under preparation in the garb of a new language and grammar based translation. The plan is being implemented through electronic media with an organized and cautious approach. Till this moment, the forum that has been exposed in this respect is the "Silsilah-e-Da'wat-e-Qurani" of respected Dr. Qamar Zaman, managing a Website and Blog by the name of "**aastana**". This humble writer has been participating in this group's academic projects for some time before the revelation of its real designs. Hence, he stands aware of the gradual internal changes that have been taking place in this forum's convictions lately.

This aspect of Islam's occult history needs serious review by the next generation of scholars. ~ oz

⚖ The Khazar Conversion

The religious conversion of the Khazars is thought to date back between the end of the 7th and the beginning of the 8th century, and is reported to have been the fruit of a deliberate decision taken within the Abrahamic world, which opted for the Jewish primacy over the cross or the crescent, to mark a net distinction between the Christian West on one side, and the East, then on its way to Islamization, on the other.

This choice was based on strategic reasons compounded with family ties and the inclusion of Jewish Radhanite merchants and a hodgepodge of other contributors from various latitudes: from Egypt to Asia Minor, from Syria to Judea, all the way to Persia and Mesopotamia. However, this did not hinder the Khaganate from engaging Muslim mercenary troops, when needed.

The conversion is prevalently attested by the "*Sefer ha-kazari*" (or "The Book of the Khazar"), written in Arabic by

♊ The Khazar Conversion

Andalusian rabbi Yehuda Ha-Levi. The decision to adopt the Jewish religion was made by the king of the time (Bulan, 737-760 AD) and was based on an in-person interview with a priest, a mullah and a rabbi. This decision is underpinned by two "reasoned instincts" of a certain relevance. The first refers to the "Constantinian" geopolitical realpolitik which would later be pursued by Vladimir the Great with the Christianization of Kievan Rus (988 AD) – a model inspired by the Khazar inclination for "active neutrality" (albeit not necessarily a peaceful one) between monotheist religions. Equally interesting, the second coincides with the will to build in Khazaria the largest possible community from the Jewish Diaspora, especially those from the Byzantine Empire.

A pole of attraction for economic, military and cultural interests, and a haven for refugees and persecuted people, the Khazar Kingdom was placed at the heart of the Silk Road (its exports, including a sizable slave trade, were bound to China and India) and was rooted in a multicultural civilization by its nature in conflict with the conquest spirit prevailing in the rest of the world.

This situation resonates with what is happening today and readers will be able to adequately ponder its effects, which may have engendered recurring cycles in history, thanks to the extremely commendable book by Giorgio Cella, who, by no coincidence, served as an OECD observer in the Ukrainian elections of 2019.

The author maintains that the Kabbalah and talmud provide legal remedies for any Jew who breaks Common Law to protect or improve the life of a Jew, including one's

⚖ The Khazar Conversion

own. Meaning Jews who murder other Jews for this purpose. The Talmud is gospel for Jewish Land Pirates, if you will, perfectly suitable for reprobate Children of Cain who'd been busy doing deep state neuro-politics for centuries. As King of Mercenaries for hire in a struggling world, it seems the Khagan may have chose wisely, but perhaps not wise enough for salvation.

♊ Annunaki

by Judge Anna Von Reiss
https://forum.alginkgo.com/go/NHIC0R6bnR

We became aware of the Anunnaki as the archeological treasures of the Middle East were unearthed; together with the later Egyptian Empires, the earlier Babylonian-Syrian Empire of the Anunnaki have provided us with a partial framework and vision of the ancient world seen through the lens of artifacts and records preserved in the strange language of Cuneiform and hieroglyphs.

Did you know that the Fleur-de-lis, the three-pronged, trident-like symbol that we associate with the Kingdom of France in modern times was once the symbol of the Anunnaki nobility, and it represented the triune kingdom of mind, body, and spirit then, just as it represents the Holy Trinity, the Unholy Trinity, and the jurisdictional realms of Land, Air, and Water (LAW) now?

A telling detail from a recent cover of the Economist magazine, the magazine cover in full, and last, but not least, a photo of an ancient bas relief carving in stone, showing the same symbol crowning one of the Anunnaki.

The Trinity in all its forms and representations is an ancient symbol of control; like the Law, it is designed to limit and control and accuse mankind, to compartmentalize our activities, and to condemn us to punishment when convenient. We see this Trinity represented in many, many venues--- religion, law, the administration of corporations; in magic; and even in the three "keys" represented on the Papal Tiara and UBS logos worldwide.

This trinity symbolism comes to us from very, very ancient sources and interestingly is not associated with the actual and factual Kingdom of Gaul—which holds the land and soil jurisdiction of what we call "France", but is instead associated with the sea jurisdiction administration and air jurisdiction that are not physically defined.

The Pattern:

England (land and soil) is redefined as "Great Britain" (sea) a business enterprise. Great Britain is redefined as "the UNITED KINGDOM" (air).

Gaul (land and soil) is redefined as "France" (sea) a business enterprise, and "France" is then redefined as "FRANCE" (air).

All this sleight of hand is used to compartmentalize and control different realms of human endeavor and provide for its tidy administrative control by a bureaucracy and forms of law that are imposed by the bureaucracy. Using this "system" of organization, it has been possible for a handful of ruling elites, who fancy themselves the progeny of the Anunnaki, to control the fates and business affairs of entire countries for generations.

Is this a token of any particular genius on the part of these gangs of criminals and their henchmen bureaucrats, or a testament to mankind's trusting and non-observant nature?

Yes, it's a nice well-organized system to divide and conquer, passed off under color of law and a facade of reasonableness, but in the end, the Trinity System, is a tool to enslave, separate, and promote elitism according to its own ancient Triune Caste System: the patricians, the indentured servants, and the slaves.

This same system adopted by the Roman Empire has, through the Church and the Commonwealth, and all associated history, been promulgated throughout the world using three separate bureaucracies and forms of law.

Imagine an ancient Robber Baron in his castle guarding a mountain pass in Germany; he has retainers and mercenaries at his command. They go out and do the dirty work for him, "arresting" travelers as they attempt to use the mountain pass he controls, and charging them passage fees, or, if they belong to certain religions or races, simply robbing them and leaving them dead in the snow.

The same thing is happening today, as members of the Municipal bureaucracy (slaves) control the jurisdiction of the air through copyrights, patents, licenses, labor contracts, and associated means, and members of the Territorial bureaucracy (indentured servants serving "tours of duty") provide muscle as mercenaries intent on controlling trade and commerce and commodities. And finally, the National bureaucracy is vacated for the convenience of the Perpetrators, who don't want to be bothered with such tiresome duties as actually running a "Kingdom" and dealing with the needs of living people.

Much more convenient to have all the living people redefined as corporation franchises, administered under forms of law intended for corporations.

These vermin only want to float along on the top of the world's proverbial punch bowl, controlling money and resources that belong to other people for their own unjust enrichment and all to the detriment of the actual owners.

It has been 8,000 years of this nonsense. Time to wake up, bring it to an end, start over with a new system — which may not be perfect, either, but at least offers the prospect of a possible different outcome.

Malcolm-X took this stand when they cut him down. ~ oz

♋ Zionism

I add the following quotes for those who may doubt the treachery of the Zionist Hierarchy:

> "It is essential that the sufferings of Jews . . . become worse . . . this will assist in realization of our plans . . . I have an excellent idea, I shall induce anti-Semites to liquidate Jewish wealth . . . The anti-Semites will assist us thereby in that they will strengthen the persecution and oppression of Jews. The anti-Semites shall be our best friends"
> Theodor Herzl, Founder of *Zionism* in *1897*

"Hateful views of Jews as being subhuman did not have to be invented by Nazi theorists such as Hitler, Goebbels, Rosenberg and Streicher. This ideology was simply adapted from statements of political Zionists... Our race is the Master Race. We are divine gods on this planet. We are as different from the inferior races as they are from insects. In fact, compared to our race, other races are beasts and animals, cattle at best. Other races are considered as human excrement. Our destiny is to rule over the inferior races. Our earthly kingdom will be ruled by our leader with a rod of iron. The masses will lick our feet and serve us as our slaves."

Menachem Begin - Israeli Prime Minister 1977–1983

Are you doubting what I say? Don't take my word, do your own investigation. It's a painful exploration but I truly believe that the balance of this planet hangs on the opening of Jewish eyes. There are many good hearted Jewish people who are being duped along with their Gentile brethren. Much of the world is waking up to the manipulations of the few and it is imperative that Jewish people join them. There is no time to waste. The information is limitless. There is no refuge for Jewish people in Israel. My dear readers, Zionism will not protect you. Zionism will crucify you on a bloody cross of avarice. It is only through a union of Jewish, Christians and Muslims that we will we be able to take back our planet.

~ Judy Andreas

"Sirs, you are doubtlessly intelligent people, however, I have a problem understanding how you found a place in prophecy for those I know to be void of a even a single drop of Hebrew blood - without any cultural or historical ties to the Holy Land and in fact simple converts to a base form of Judaism. Clinton eulogized Rabinowitz (Yitzhak Rabin) as a son of David and a son of Solomon. You must know that this man was a Khazar of Turko-Mongolian lineage, and can in no way represent a 'return' since his southern Russian ancestors never made it down to Palestine until 1948."

~ David Hunt (author), in a radio interview, 2007

SEE: Rodrique, A (2000).
Sephardi Jewry: A History of the Judeo-Spanish
Community, *14th-20th Centuries (Jewish Communities in the Modern World)*. University of California Press. *I*SBN 978-0520218222. OCLC 154877054

The Iron Curtain Over America, John Beatty, Eleventh Printing April 1954.

This volume provides a complete history of East European Jewry—of the Khazars—a people [Gog] who converted to Judaism in the 9th Cent AD and adopted the *Babylonian Talmud*. These are those who have no genealogical ties to any Israeli Tribe and yet many have become Chiefs of Zionism and the Illuminati. They are self-styled Sephardim and inimical Crypto-Jews; enemies to all men.

Acknowledgments

Such a cloud of witnesses !
Where to begin ?
where to end ?
I cannot say.

Although I am grateful to all readers, my closest neighbor makes the path easy for me, so that each day is greeted afresh with delight and mutual esteem for the purposes of our joint venture. The latter were made clear to us in dreams, both individually and collectively, and now, historically.

Of such is the wedded grace described in this book, which I humbly lay at her feet.

Thank you Amina Qun Gu, my dear heart.

About the Author

Omar Zaid is a retired medical doctor who lived in SE Asia from 2000 to 2021 where he held senior lecturer and research fellow chairs. He now holds the honorable old man's seat at Al Ginkgo Farm, in Liberty, Kentucky.

Ms Amina Gu, is the right honorable lady of the farm. Together, we live what this book describes, so don't hesitate to contact us if sincerely interested in our testimony.

My several books on the occult histories of metaphysics and theology will likely change your worldview.

Thank you kindly.

write to info@alginkgo.com
https://www.alginkgo.com
https://forum.alginkgo.com/go/8eMpCJlHnD

Also By Dr. Zaid

https://forum.alginkgo.com/go/CCrRrtxSlH

CAIN'S CREED

"If ever there was a body of men who merited damnation on earth and in hell, it is this Society of Loyola,"

John Quincy Adams

Dr Zaid exposes the interconnected webs of hidden cabals by connecting known and unknown dots. He takes us to Roman-Britain where Church ritual began to craft its present form; and from there to a Medieval Pope who caused all clergy to divorce their wives; and then to Jesuits who forever seek war and to finance all sides in tandem with the Jews who founded them as well as the early Flavian Church.

Cain's Creed is *rich reading* for all who treasure the hidden histories of Christendom and the Papacy. But it is *must reading* for those who claim to be informed. Only by understanding your enemy can you determine a strategy that protects and defends yourself and whomever Allah assigns to your right hand.

sister klara, singapore, 2024

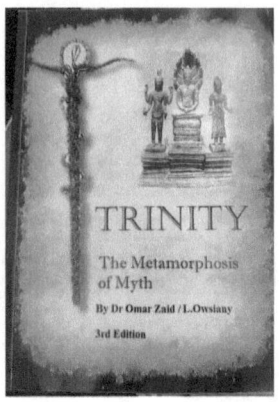

TRINITY: The Metamorphosis of Myth

https://forum.alginkgo.com/go/9z3fNJopca

Trinity is a thorough critique of all strands of thought of all ages which, in the author's view, have helped in one way or another to corrupt the tenets of pure monotheism. This book must be published. - Prof. Dato Dr. Osman Bakar

Trinity' is an ambitious and provocative critique—a 'small plate of meaty polemic with a hot relish of reason', as the author asserts—that focuses on the so-called facts, theories and philosophical ideals behind various religious faiths, with a particular spotlight on Islam, which Zaid, as a staunch Muslim, defends with conviction – though not uncritically. Zaid is an erudite writer who explores his subjects with a verve and infectious curiosity born of interest, sincerity and certainty.

- *Literary Review*, London, (2006)

After reading Trinity I couldn't sleep until I became a muslim. ~ The Late Francis Yeoh, KL, Malaysia, 2008.

Trinity *is a fierce denunciation of the myths that surround many religions. At the same time, it explains why the One*

God is such a compelling belief in a simple, down-to-earth manner. This is what makes this unique book so attractive.

- Prof. Dr. Chandra Muzaffar

SEXOLOGY for the wise
https://forum.alginkgo.com/go/NTzOMIeg2i

This essay collection applies wide-ranging optics to myths of LGBT fidelity and normality. The author compares and contrasts biological, metaphysical, psychological, moral, and social domains and dynamics that define and delimit normative heterosexual duality with those of the gender-confused. He does this in terms that illustrate and justify spiritual and physical absolutes that are denied yet manipulated by postmodern nihilists and oligarchs of the occult governance that institutionalizes evil.

The heterosexual dyad is rigorously defended *as basal, cardinal, essential, naturally hegemonic, and not the least bit ambiguous.*

No one has approached the topic with such verve or comprehensive acumen. Dr. Zaid's all-embracing synthesis is both frightening and fascinating. He leaves nothing untouched in this race through the Holocene. So effective is his insight that the reader's world view is irremediably shaken and changed. Religion, Theology, Scripture, History, Science,

Geo-Politics, Human Nature, Magick, Philosophy and Occult Mystery Systems are blended in an intense dot-connecting narrative that crosses all bounds of taboo to reveal much we do not wish to acknowledge.

Beware. Do not proceed *unless you are prepared to transcend mundane religious and socio-political indoctrinations.*

TRUST: Ontogeny & Misplacement

https://forum.alginkgo.com/go/yPWVkBwKXF

Learn how it naturally develops and how it is destroyed. Dr Zaid throttles all psycho babble. His ability for gestalt assimilation and synthesis cures confusion and eases the troubled heart. Elegant, deeply insightful, and rich in references that irrefutably indicate a longstanding scheme to brainwash and enslave us like cattle.

YOUR CLOSEST NEIGHBOR

A MANUAL FOR THE RIGHTLY GUIDED

the seven basic needs of your spouse

https://forum.alginkgo.com/go/2VzHog7xVJ

Wisdom doesn't get better than this. This book describes seven fundamental emotional and psychic needs for men and women. Other gender identities are not discussed, but they too will benefit from the wisdom presented. These gendered needs are described for each spouse in two separate chapters. You will be interested to know what they are, aren't, and how they differ. Dr. Zaid then presents a very convincing pan-scriptural essay that describes the purpose of marriage. If you want to acknowledge the divine in your marriage, and do this consciously together with your loved one. Buy this book. Read it. Keep it as a bedside companion.

―――

for others see: https://forum.alginkgo.com/go/837uVmTHbd

www.ingramcontent.com/pod-product-compliance
Lightning Source LLC
Chambersburg PA
CBHW022019220426
43663CB00007B/1136